The End of Emily West

Wendy Turner Webster

AuthorHouse™ UK Ltd.
500 Avebury Boulevard
Central Milton Keynes, MK9 2BE
www.authorhouse.co.uk
Phone: 08001974150

© 2009 Wendy Turner Webster. All rights reserved.

No part of this book may be reproduced, stored in a retrieval system, or transmitted by any means without the written permission of the author.

First published by AuthorHouse 6/10/2009

ISBN: 978-1-4389-8666-1 (sc)
ISBN: 978-1-4389-8667-8 (hc)

This book is printed on acid-free paper.

For Gary, Jack and Freddie

*With special thanks to Jeanette Fuller for
your unfailing support and faith.*

*Thank you to Sandra Horley, Lisa King and Janqui Mehta
at Refuge for your wonderful input and enthusiasm.*

*Thank you to Cherie Booth QC, Patron of
Refuge, for the front cover quote.*

*With huge thanks to Doreen M Langhorn SWA for allowing
me to use her stunning painting, 'The Red Bucket'.*

And with grateful thanks always to John Elkin

Author's Introduction

WHILST THE END OF EMILY WEST is, in essence, a work of fiction I have based the elements of domestic violence on true events in my own life. Most significantly, inspiration for the character of Darren O'Dowel was drawn from my own experiences during my first marriage. I have chosen the title to reflect the fact that when one emerges from a violent relationship it is very much 'the end' of you as that person; it is the end of one life and, if you are to be a survivor and not a victim, a new life must inevitably begin.

When I used to film Pet Rescue I came into contact with many animals of all shapes, sizes and dispositions... when giving interviews at that time I used to make a joke of the fact that during any given filming day I may be bitten, kicked, head-butted or in the case of one particularly bad-tempered Llama, spat upon! In actual fact all those things had happed to me before in a life which was a far cry from the glitz and glamour of television; a life filled with violence, fear and shame. I suppose on the theme of animals I could compare myself to a mouse back in those days – a very scared and lonely mouse shivering and cowering in a corner – not daring to come out or even make a squeak for fear of abuse.

I lived on a knife edge too for the fact that he might explode at any time, and over any small thing… Tiredness, a long day at the office, a drink, a casual or innocent comment from me may all trigger an explosive episode. I may be slapped or kicked to the floor, I may be given a spiteful pinch or maybe a vicious punch in the back to catapult me out of the bed. On some occasions I would get back into the bed only to be woken up later by having a bucket of water poured over me. Once, I had the presence of mind to lock myself in the bedroom but this didn't keep him at bay for too long. If I didn't open the door he was going to break it down with an axe. I remember looking out of the window and considering whether I would survive the jump. I thought not and so opened the door.

I think I lost count of how many times I would be made to beg for mercy – my face crushed into the carpet with an arm forced up behind my back. The last time an incident such as that happened he wrapped his hands around my throat and screamed that this time he really was going to kill me… unless of course I begged to be allowed to live.

So how did all these things make me feel? Worthless, stupid, lonely, frightened, suicidal, humiliated, without dignity, without strength and without the confidence or presence of mind to extract myself from the pit of despair I found myself in. I stayed because I didn't have the mental capability to get out. I became utterly reliant upon David, totally brainwashed into thinking that I needed him to survive, that his temper was always induced by me, that it was all my fault and that I couldn't stand on my own two feet without him. In fact, eventually, he left me and I clearly remember lying in a crumpled heap in the doorway begging him to stay. His parting shot was, *I may come back to you if I need some shirts ironing.*

The abuse I suffered seems so far away now, so distant from my lovely life with my fabulous husband Gary and our two beautiful boys and I must admit is it a painful experience for me to dredge up that past and re-live the memories. I would prefer to keep the pain and the humiliation hidden away in a little box, never to see the light of day again. However, that would be of little use to the thousands of women out there who are suffering and several years ago, with Gary's strength of support, I made up my mind to talk about what had happened to me in an effort to raise awareness of the subject and to help carry on and fund the vital work done by Refuge. I also realised that I was a pretty good example of the fact that there is a life to be had beyond the abuse, a life in fact which is absolutely worth living.

At this very moment in time, whilst you are reading this introduction, a woman is being violently abused by her partner. At this minute the bruises are already turning purple, the blood is already flowing and she is begging her partner to stop. She is alone and frightened and yet another victim.

With any luck, and sooner rather than later, she will be taken under the wonderful wing of Refuge. She will not believe it yet, whilst the bruises are still fresh, but in time, with Refuge's help, she will recover, build a new life and have new dreams… she may even regain her confidence to such an extent that in a few years time she will be able to stand up and talk about her experiences, as I have done.

I hope that you can read The End of Emily West and take inspiration from it – specifically to join the fight against the unacceptable crime of domestic violence.

Wendy Turner Webster

Foreword

Sandra Horley, OBE, chief executive of Refuge, national domestic violence charity

DOMESTIC VIOLENCE IS A CRIME. It takes lives and it shatters lives. Everyday in this country thousands of women like the character Emily West are living with the terror of domestic violence – two women a week are killed in England and Wales by a current or former partner.

I would like to congratulate Wendy Turner Webster for her courage in speaking out about domestic violence. 'The End of Emily West' will undoubtedly reach out to thousands of abused women and encourage them to seek help from organisations like Refuge. This novel will show women that they are not alone and that there are many women experiencing domestic violence every day of their lives. Like Wendy, who has a successful career and a fulfilling life and who is very happily married to Gary, all women have the right to live a life free from violence.

Many abused women reading this book are likely to sympathise with Emily West and may feel responsible for and ashamed of the violence. Let me be absolutely clear, no one is to blame for another person's behaviour. Violence is a choice and men who abuse women must take responsibility for their actions.

Wendy's portrayal of the character Darren O'Dowel is typical of so many abusive men. From the outset Darren is charming and likeable, but soon his behaviour changes and he becomes controlling, jealous and possessive. Over time his abusive behaviour increases in frequency and severity. Sadly for many women who experience domestic violence threats to their life are all too common – luckily in this book Emily manages to escape an attack on her life, although only just.

Anyone reading this book may try to blame Darren's behaviour on alcohol – but alcohol is only an excuse to be violent. As Wendy shows readers time after time, Darren is just as likely to be abusive both mentally and physically whether he's drunk or stone cold sober.

Over time Darren gradually erodes Emily's confidence - like water dripping on a stone. In spite of all the obstacles in her way, Emily survived a dangerous and stressful situation.

Refuge is committed to a world where abuse does not exist and where domestic violence is unacceptable behaviour. Refuge provides emergency life saving and life changing domestic violence services and campaigns to challenge negative attitudes to bring about positive and enduring change.

I have no doubt that The End of Emily West will give a message of great hope to the thousands of women who will read this book. Wendy Turner Webster's words will help Refuge break the isolation that so many abused women and children live with on a daily basis and in so doing will help save lives.

I would urge any woman experiencing domestic violence to get in touch with Refuge – it is a brave and positive first step to receiving the support and protection she needs and deserves. Or, if you are reading this and think that someone you know is being abused – a friend, a daughter, a sister, or a colleague – contact Refuge. It could save a life.

Domestic violence is a crime. Don't ignore it - everyone has a responsibility to challenge violence. And from all at Refuge, a big thank you to Wendy for sharing some of her personal experience and for helping us to bring domestic violence from behind closed doors.

Visit www.refuge.org.uk to find out more to access support and find out about Refuge's work. Why not sign up to the Refuge monthly newsletter? Or to find out how you can help raise money? Domestic violence is an issue that affects us all – get involved and play your part in helping bring an end to this devastating crime.

The Beginning

Chapter 1

NOTHING CAN BE WORSE FOR A mother than losing her child. This was the thought running through the mind of eleven year old Emily West as she watched her mum drop to her knees at the graveside of little Bobby, rocking back and forth in her own private hell. Emily knelt beside her and saw the steady flow of tears splash down onto the pink granite of the grave. The tears were unchecked and the quiet sobbing that accompanied them was pitiful. Even the hardest person could not fail to be moved by such obvious grief. But still Emily did not cry. Years later she was to look back and realise that she was simply too shocked to cry, to make such a show of raw emotion, to add her tears to those of her parents. She felt sad, empty and detached from the devastation around her. A horrible kind of nothingness that made her heart feel like lead and kept her bright hazel eyes stone dry.

In the distance she saw her dad standing by the wall mounted tap just inside the churchyard gates. He filled a bucket with water for the purple heathers that they'd planted on the grave, a tribute to the fact that Bobby's very favourite colour in the whole wide world was purple. Before walking over to join them Emily saw him blowing his nose into a giant white hanky then stuff it deep into the pocket of his brown corduroy trousers. It occurred to her then that before Bobby's death she had never witnessed her dad crying. Why should she? The

West family were four happy, carefree and contented people. They had two cars, a nice house, a pony, holidays every year and food on the table. Now, in St Matthew's churchyard on a sunny August afternoon during the hottest summer for 46 years, their tight knit family unit had finally fallen apart. Their youngest member lay dead and cold and hard beneath the earth. That beautifully formed, blonde-haired six year old little boy who was loved and adored by everyone who knew him had had his life snatched away from him in what seemed like the blinking of an eye. Her strong, jovial, lover-of-life father had visibly shrunk over the past week. Part of his very soul had left this earth along with that of his only son, and in a moment of panic Emily truly believed that she'd never see her parents laugh or even smile ever again.

As her dad's stooped frame walked slowly towards them, Emily looked past her mother to the gold inscription on the headstone. *Robert George West, Born April 25th 1970, died July 31st 1976. Beloved son of Maria and William and baby brother to Emily. Darling Bobby, The Joy You Brought Us We Shall Never Forget.* Such beautiful, truthful words. And she noticed for the first time how much the pink granite sparkled in the sunlight, as if set with the same diamond chips of her favourite ring.

It was amazing thought Emily, how people managed to survive such an onslaught of grief and pain… you could have such a massive dose of tragedy and unbearable heartache that you truly believed that the world was coming to an end. It was as if the whole planet should be paralysed with you; go into a voluntary freeze because the pain of existing in it was too great a burden to bear. But when you woke up in the morning it was almost a shock to find that the world was still turning. I'm bigger then you, it seemed to gloat… your enormous grief that has brought you to the brink of madness cannot compete with me, for whatever happens to you and your kind I shall still be here, turning, turning, turning.

Emily pondered on the fact that it was of course your own little world that stopped turning, ceased to function, willingly giving up all rights to future happiness. It was the little world in your head that froze, the one that gave you your mind, your character, your soul. Emily didn't realise it then but the thoughts that summed up her anxiety, grief and loneliness had already begun burrowing, worming, clawing… clinging on to her brain like parasites that would never let go.

It's funny how life just goes on, she thought, realising with a large pang of guilt that she felt really hungry. Little Bobby was dead and all she could think about was her stomach! But she would have to eat. Sooner or later her parents would have to eat also. The gas bill would have to be paid, clothes would have to be washed and ironed, the garden would have to be weeded and slowly but surely smiles would have to form on their faces and spontaneous laughter would have to come from their hearts. But not yet. At the moment they were all still falling apart, slowly dying themselves in a neat little countryside graveyard, thinking of the angelic little boy who would never grow old.

Emily looked across the graves and elaborate tombs to the field beyond where a man in shirt sleeves and a flat cap was chugging up and down on a sit-on mower, a little white terrier yapping at the wheels. The dog sounded like it was wildly excited, having the time of its life. The man looked content, in control, satisfied with his work. They were happy; a happy little team tending the land and at that moment in time Emily would have given anything to be either one of them. The hum of the mower was strangely soothing as it drifted towards them and the sweet smell of freshly mown grass reminded Emily of the recent summer sports day at school. How a smell can instantly transport a person to another time, a different place. As Emily closed her eyes and inhaled the summer air she was back on the school playing field, reliving that glorious moment where she had won the hundred meter dash: broken through the finish tape and felt for one amazing, magical moment that there wasn't a thing in the world that she couldn't achieve.

"…love… Emily, love… come on. Let's get ourselves back home."
Emily's eyes snapped open and squinting through the harsh sunlight she realised her dad was beckoning her to head for the car. Her mum was on her feet and being lead away; her head was still bent, the tears were still flowing but dad's comforting arm was around her

shoulders guiding her towards the wrought iron gates and out into the car park. Emily trailed behind miserably, stealing one last look at Bobby's grave, suddenly missing his wet, sugary kisses and high-pitched giggles so acutely it almost took her breath away. Climbing into the car she caught a glimpse of the man in the field getting off his mower. He stooped down and picked up a stick, then sent it spinning through the air. The white terrier went into a mad frenzy, barking and yapping and tearing after the piece of wood as if his life depended on it, his fast little heels kicking up the freshly mown grass, sending it in all directions before it fluttered back down to the ground. As they drove away from St Matthew's Emily thought with some bitterness that her beautiful memory of the school sports day was now tainted for ever - that for the rest of her life the sweet summery smell of freshly cut grass would not remind her of the hundred meters win, but would always be linked with the graveside memories of this most dreadful day, and missing Bobby so much that it hurt.

Chapter 2

ROBERT GEORGE WEST WAS BORN ON 25th April 1970 at ten past seven in the morning. He came a full two weeks earlier than expected and when Emily's dad bundled her and her mother into the car at just turned midnight she shivered with an equal mixture of cold and excitement. Emily was five years old and had wanted a baby brother or sister for as long as she could remember – a wish that Maria and William West had found hard to grant. Conceiving Emily seemed to have taken no effort at all; a traditional wedding with all the trimmings, a honeymoon in the Highlands, the setting up of a new home in Shropshire and bingo! Married for just four months before Dr Drake confirmed that a baby was indeed on the way. It had been so easy and so taken for granted that when, three years later, they decided to add to their brood, Maria and William had no doubts at all that a new bundle of joy would be instantly forthcoming. It wasn't. After three months Maria started to worry and after seven months they were both tormenting themselves with the fact that they may never have another child. Making love became an act of desperation. Maria would cry inconsolably when a few drops of blood confirmed that yet another month of vigorous sexual activity had not brought the desired result and William would take her in his arms, unable to find the words to bring about any ounce of comfort or consolation.

They went to see Dr Drake for the obligatory tests, resisting the temptation to blame each other for the distinct lack of swelling around Maria's slender waist. She had *lost* weight if anything; unable to face breakfast if she had seen a new born baby whilst doing the nursery run with Emily, picking at her lunch if a morning visit to the Post Office had featured a little one in a pram.

"What *is* it, doctor?" asked William as they sat in the surgery, eager yet at the same time dreading to hear the results of the recent tests. "Is it me? Is it Maria? What on earth are we doing wrong? It was so easy last time, with Emily… what's so different now?"

Dr Drake looked briefly from one to the other and felt a familiar pang of sorrow. If only people realised how common this was, to have a baby with all the ease of slipping on ice only to come to a grinding halt when they wanted another one. The unnecessary strain it put on a relationship was all too evident with the couple who sat before him. William's face was pale, pinched and strained and Maria was far too thin. At this moment in time she reminded Dr Drake very much of an undernourished, frightened rabbit; her eyes were too wide and bright as they darted nervously around the room and she twitched about restlessly on the edge of her seat. Thank God in this case he could give them some hope, all the hope in the world in fact as the test results showed that there was absolutely nothing to prevent Maria and William from having another baby quite naturally. They must go home, relax, eat well, sleep well and not worry and in the fullness of time Dr Drake was sure that Baby West would surprise them all and come into being.

And so the months went by. They followed Dr Drake's advice; had early nights, ate good food and tried to relax about the whole 'baby issue'. To their credit they didn't let their longing for another baby overshadow their love for Emily and she was lavished with so much care and attention that sometimes when they both tiptoed into her room and gazed down upon her sleeping form they thought their hearts might burst with love and pride. Two years later, when Emily was five, Maria and William had just about given up hope of ever being more than a family of three. Emily was about to start her first term at primary school and their minds were focused fully on school shoes, school bags and remembering the name of the Head Mistress and Form Teacher. The first day of term of the new school year was somewhat overcast but thankfully dry and William ushered Emily and Maria out into the garden to take pictures. There was still plenty of colour in the garden. The summer had been a good one with August in particular boasting long summer days and balmy evenings, followed often by thundery nights which drenched the garden and made the flowers bloom like they'd never bloomed before. Emily stood proudly in her new school uniform, the snowy white shirt tucked neatly into the navy blue pleated skirt, legs like two little pink sticks standing in a pair of shiny grey lace-up shoes. Maria straightened the grey and navy boater hat, making sure that the position of the green and grey embroidered school badge was dead centre. 'Veritas' it declared. 'Truth' Maria had explained to Emily, "Always tell the truth unless it's kinder to tell a little white lie!"

Purple and lilac pansies cascaded from a hanging basket on Emily's left and behind her dozens of pink and lilac lupins stood side by side like soldiers on parade. A creamy white clematis twisted and snaked its way around a small leylandii tree, covering the dark green foliage, threatening to choke and smother it until one's eyes could be deceived into thinking there was no leylandii tree there at all. William took eight photographs, coaxing Emily into different poses until she finally complained that staring into the camera for so long was making her eyes water. The flowers and plants that had never looked more luscious than on that cool September morning had provided the perfect frame for a picture of their perfect little girl and one of the photographs from that special photo shoot stayed in William's wallet until the day he died. The photo would fade and the edges would wrinkle but the little girl with the Veritas badge shone out of the picture with a light so bright it would be hard to extinguish.

Maria hadn't paid any attention to her monthly cycle for some time when she realised that it was possible, just possible that she may be pregnant. The monthly anguish and gnawing of fingers in anticipation of the sign she longed for had ceased a long time ago and a complete devotion to Emily had replaced, she thought, her craving for another child. Maria and William counted their blessings, took and accepted what the fates dealt out and thanked their lucky stars that they had at least had one beautiful baby.

"After all", Maria would say to anyone who was interested, "Some women can't have *any* children…"

And William's contribution was, "We've got *one* beautiful little girl you know… mustn't be greedy!"

Yet when Maria returned from the doctor's with the news that a miracle had happened, that she was indeed pregnant and they could expect a baby to be born in May of the following year, they both realised they had been kidding themselves. When the full impact of the news hit them they went into emotional overdrive and wanted this baby desperately, more desperately and urgently than they could ever have imagined. Emily was ecstatic. All the dolls in the world could not compare to a real, live, burping and giggling baby; a living doll that needed milk all the time and its nappy changing every hour. It would need cuddles too… and walks in the pram… tiny little clothes and lots of different coloured booties! Emily too went into emotional overdrive and all three members of the West family waited with obvious and gleeful impatience for the following spring.

By the time the daffodils and crocuses were nosing through the earth, searching for sunlight, names had been chosen; Robert George for a boy and Amelia Jane for a girl. By the time the egg hunts were over and clouds of cherry blossom were covering the trees in their road, the third bedroom in the West's house had been transformed into a nursery. As neither pink nor blue could be used with any degree of certainty, Maria had gone for whites and creams, primrose yellows and soft apple greens. Secretly Emily was hoping for a baby brother and had a blurred vision of blue, a little bundle of blue with fat chubby legs and sky blue eyes that would gaze upon his older sister and adore her instantly. When at last the baby was born, her prayers were answered.

When Emily went into school the day after Bobby's early arrival, the class teacher, Mrs Ellery, asked her to stand up and tell the class 'in a big loud voice' what she had been up to the day before. The bespectacled teacher, with sandy hair down to her waist and a wide skirt down to the floor tilted her head on one side and smiled affectionately as Emily, shy at being the sudden focus of attention, retold the adventure of the last twenty four hours. After the first few sentences she gained some confidence and by the end of the story she was fully in command, holding the gaze of each class member and feeling at least two inches taller than when she had started. For a few minutes she had held an audience in the hollow of her hand and it gave her a warm, heady feeling she hoped she'd never forget. As she sat down and the class began to copy the alphabet from the blackboard into their exercise books, Mrs Ellery gave an inward sigh and wondered what the years would hold for Emily West. What had life got in store for the five year old girl who could light up the classroom, whose absence was felt immediately if a cough or a cold (or a baby brother even) had prevented her from attending school?

Barbara Ellery had been a teacher for some thirty three years and every once in a while a new intake of pupils would throw up a gem; a little boy or girl who, if you could, you would definitely refer to as your 'favourite'. Of course favouritism was strongly discouraged and hardly ever admitted to but as a teacher you simply couldn't help being inexplicably drawn to some children and not feeling anything in particular about others. Mrs Ellery often felt surges of affection towards Emily. She was articulate, willing and able. She was happy, cheeky and full of fun. She was kind to others and shared herself out in the playground when more than one of her classmates was making demands upon her friendship. And those eyes! Wide hazel eyes with lashes that any grown woman would surely kill for.

When the bell went for the morning break and the whole class surged towards the door and out into the playground, Mrs Ellery sat behind her desk for a few moments and quietly let her mind drift. For some inexplicable reason she suddenly felt rather old. How many hundreds of children had she taught over the years? How much energy had she given? Energy, love, patience and compassion… and she had watched on in delight as all the little people in her care had absorbed information like sponges. She had given them the foundation of knowledge, the very lifeblood of progress; ABCs and one, two, threes and sent them off at the end of that precious first year with a hunger for more. But whatever became of them? What was the fate of those sweet little rascals, all those hundreds of blank pages waiting for something meaningful to be written on them? Mrs Ellery gave herself an inward shake and sternly reminded herself that one couldn't possibly keep a track of all the pupils one came into contact with. It was impossible, silly to even think about it. She mustn't think about it. Moreover it was quite ridiculous to sit here in the classroom and get melancholy about it. But as she started to catch up with some marking the feeling stayed with her and she put down her pencil and her gold star stickers with a frustrated sigh. It was Emily's little speech this morning she supposed that had brought the memories back. It was thinking about that dear little girl and inwardly praying that life would be kind to her. For she could tell even now that Emily was not destined to have an easy time. People who sparkled in quite the way she did rarely took the easy route; they wanted challenges, adventure, danger even. They didn't want ordinary jobs or sensible partners or ordinary / sensible anything for that matter. She *feared* for Emily and it was at that point that she gave in and admitted to herself the real reason for her sad and sombre mood. She battled to suppress the memory but it was too strong, too vivid. Christopher May - little Christopher May who she had been reminded of the minute Emily described her baby brother's shock of blond hair and startling blue eyes. She tried never to think of Christopher May. Several years ago he too had been one of her 'favourites'. He too had been destined never to settle for the usual, the mundane. Unlike many of her other pupils though Christopher had kept in touch with her after his reception year was over, making it his business to seek her out and say hello. When eventually he left the junior school he brought her a painting he'd done of the school and she had promised faithfully to frame it. She still had the painting but it had never been framed, never taken pride of place on her wall. Christopher left the school in the summer and over the holidays Barbara was surprised to open up the local paper and see his face staring out at her. Christopher was missing, his family were distraught, the police were out searching for him. But wherever he had gone, whatever had become of him, no one ever found out. Missing? Murdered? Run away? Abducted? Christopher May, from that day to this, had never been seen or heard of again. And as the school bell rang and Emily lead her little gaggle of friends back into the classroom, Barbara Ellery had a sudden reckless and savage urge to wave a magic wand over all these little children and cast a spell which ensured they would never have to grow up.

Chapter 3

DRIVING HOME FROM ST MATTHEW'S CHURCHYARD, Emily thought once again of the small terrier dog, yapping and snapping at the wheels of the mower. She thought of the water tap her dad had used and of the thousands of people who must have trudged back and forth from the tap to the graves. And she thought about a particularly impressive tomb they had passed to get to Bobby's patch and wondered about the remains that lay within. In fact she spent the entire journey trying to think about anything other than the empty space beside her in the back seat. At a zebra crossing they stopped to let a small girl and presumably her mother cross the road. The girl was pushing a shiny new bike, all pink and chrome with ribbons streaming from the handle bars. She was giggling about something and the lady who was with her reached down and ruffled her hair before they both skipped the last couple of yards to the pavement. Emily suddenly hated the carefree little girl with the brand new bike and the happy smiling mother. What on earth were they laughing about? What gave them the right to not have a care in the world and to do silly skips across the road to prove it? The bitterness she felt threatened to overwhelm her, to make her choke with rage and she dug her finger nails into her knees to try and make the feeling go away.

"All right, love?" her dad asked, glancing over his shoulder as he put the car into first gear and set off again.

"Yes thanks, dad," she replied. But the words sounded silly and high pitched, too bright and cheerful and she dug her nails deeper into her flesh.

William gently touched Maria on the forearm. "Are you OK love?"

"Yes…"

"My God, just look at the new Burlington Court flats – they've shot up quickly!"

"Yes…"

"Someone'll make a tidy sum out of that lot."

"Yes…"

"I'll make us some sandwiches when we get home… then why don't you go and lie down for an hour or so love? Have a rest…"

"Yes…"

Emily wanted to scream. *Yes, yes, yes, yes, yes!* Was there no other word to say? Was there no other response to give? He's dead, *dead*, and you're talking about flats and sandwiches and rests and saying *yes, yes, yes*. But there were no screams, no tantrums, no embarrassing outbursts. William's forced cheerfulness turned into silence and he concentrated on the road ahead. Maria retreated into her self imposed shell and gazed into her lap, then began picking mindlessly at a loose thread hanging from the hem of her skirt. Emily stared at the back of her mum's head and realised that she'd never seen her hair quite so messy and tangled. A couple of minutes later they were pulling into the drive of their home, Oakside Grange, and as William turned off the car engine, Emily was momentarily shocked to look down and see thin trails of blood running down her knees.

William did make sandwiches, although they were only briefly nibbled at, and Maria did go up to their bedroom for an afternoon rest. William said that he had some paperwork he should be getting on with (after all, the office had been very understanding over the past couple of weeks) and he would be in the study if anyone needed him. *I need you*, a voice inside Emily screamed although in contrast she gave a bright smile and said that that was fine because she was going down to the field to take Rascal some carrots.

It was only a ten minute walk to Rascal's field at Whitemoor Farm and Emily set off to see her beloved pony armed with a bag full of carrots and his red head collar and lead rein slung over her shoulder. In the blazing heat of that afternoon the lane was dusty and dry. Crackling noises came from the hedgerows as various wildlife went about its business within the maze of parched branches, and high above in the cloudless sky a small aeroplane flew to some far off land. Emily turned into the driveway which led into the small stable yard. Old Mr Harvey, who owned the stables and the adjoining white, rather tumbledown cottage, was up a ladder doing some minor repairs to the cottage guttering.

He turned from his work. "Hello Emily!"

"Hi, Mr Harvey…"

"Not riding in this blinkin' heat are you love?!"

"No… just brought some carrots… and Rascal's probably covered in dust so I'll give him a good brush."

"Right you are. Mrs Harvey cleaned all the brushes last night so they're all spick and span in the tack room ready to go. Last saw Rascal with Buttons and Starlight under the big Sycamore…"

"Thank you!" Emily shouted back, and climbed over the five barred gate to head for the shade of the Sycamore tree.

Poor little bugger, thought Mr Harvey as he teetered about precariously at the top of his ladders. How she must miss him… and putting such a brave face on it. Her and that little Bobby had been joined at the hip! The times they'd both come down here and played about with Rascal… her trying to be a serious horsewoman and him just wanting to play cowboys and Indians. Bloomin' 'eck, life wasn't fair, was it? Not one little bit. How that poor little boy could have gone like that… my God, he'd only been down here at the stables a matter of hours before it happened. Mrs Harvey had wept buckets and he'd shed a fair few tears himself if truth be told. Damn, he'd be welling up again now if he didn't stop thinking about it. What time was it anyway? Surely it was time for a break, a nice cup of tea? Anyway it was too bloody hot to be up a pair of ladders for long. Using the heat and his desire for a cup of tea as the excuse, Mr Harvey started to climb down his ladders, but not before angrily brushing away a tear that was making its way down his old leathery face.

Rascal, Buttons and Starlight had indeed taken refuge under the large Sycamore tree. All three of them stood with drooping heads and heavy eyes, their tails constantly flicking away the summer flies, the only living creatures that seemed to have any energy at all in this insufferable heat. The bag of carrots was met with cool indifference and eventually Emily flopped down and leant against the tree trunk, too tired and too hot to trudge back up the field to collect the clean brushes from the tack room. Rascal's beautiful chestnut coat lay hidden under a fine layer of dust, and for the first time since his arrival Emily felt too tired to care.

If Emily was to look back on her childhood, it was the spring and early summer before Bobby died that stood out as a golden and perfect time. Not that long ago if you looked at it on a calendar - barely three months in fact since Rascal had burst on to the scene - but a lifetime in terms of events, triumphs and tragedies. In the heat of that lazy afternoon spent under the Sycamore tree, Emily allowed herself the luxury of reliving those glorious months, savouring the happy memories... and wishing that the story could have had a different ending....

Chapter 4

"Bobby… Bobby! Come here!" shouted Emily. "Your bath's ready!"

Having bathed herself and already in her red and pink stripped pyjamas, Emily threw a few of Bobby's favourite toys into the tub and shouted him again.

"Come *on* Bobby, I've got something to whisper to you!"

The lure of some secret whispering worked and Bobby came bounding up the stairs, ripping off his clothes on the way.

"Secrets! Secrets! What is it? *Please* tell me Emy…"

"Get into the bath quickly then because I want to shout Dad up here," said Emily. And then with lips pressed up to Bobby's ear she revealed her plan. "Let's ask Dad if we can have a pony!"

Bobby giggled and stared at his sister with blue eyes as wide as saucers.

"A *pony*…? Do you really think he'll say yes..?

"I don't know Bobby… not really I suppose but we can try can't we? I mean, if not this summer Mum and Dad could think about it for *next* summer perhaps…"

William West followed the call up the stairs and sat himself down on the bath mat beside Emily. Two expectant faces gazed up at him.

"You two are up to something," he said, with the usual twinkle in his eye, "Come on, out with it!"

"Go on Emy," urged Bobby, "Ask Daddy about a pony!"

"A pony?!" repeated William "What about a pony?"

"Well, Dad..." began Emily, glaring at Bobby, "I was wondering, well *we* were wondering... if we could maybe... one day have... well, have a pony?"

Once again two little faces stared at William, daring to be hopeful but already preparing for the crushing disappointment of the word 'no'.

"Well," said William slowly, "I don't see why not... Old Mrs Dooley's got some land she may rent out... and there's Whitemoor Farm down the way... might be worth having a word with Mr and Mrs Harvey... they may rent us a field and a stable. Yes... Hell, YES, let's get you two a pony!"

So many whoops and screams and cries of laughter and delight came from the bathroom that Maria came rushing in to see what all the fuss was about.

"A pony, Mum!" shouted Emily, "We're getting a *pony*! Can you believe it?!"

William was doing a jig with Emily around the bathroom, pleased as punch to be the source of so much joy. After all, isn't that what he and Maria lived for, to bring joy and warmth and laughter to their precious son and daughter?

"No, I can't believe it," said Maria frowning. "Come on William, none of us know the first thing about ponies!"

"Then we'll just have to learn, won't we love?"

And with those brave words ringing in their ears, the West family set about finding a pony, a stable and a field and amassing all the knowledge they could about the principles of horsemanship. To the children's bitter disappointment enquiries to Mrs Dooley brought news of an already full stable yard, which made a thumbs up from Mr and Mrs Harvey all the more reason to celebrate. Not only did they have enough land and accommodation for one more pony (they had two already), but they also knew of a suitable pony for sale.

"Aye, John Tiller over at Ditton Bridge has got a grand little chestnut gelding for sale. His Caroline's fifteen now and far more interested in boys than horses! Let's see... pony must be about thirteen hands high I reckon. Just right for your two."

William had no idea what 'thirteen hands high' meant but Emily assured him that it was perfect. She had only been to one lesson at the local riding school by the time they made the journey over to Ditton Bridge and she felt slightly foolish at not being able to put the pony through his paces.

"Never mind," said Caroline, "Keep having those riding lessons and you'll master it in no time. Anyway, he's very safe. A lorry going past spitting out firecrackers wouldn't phase our Rascal, would it boy?"

And so a deal was struck. Eight year old Welsh Arab cross Rascal was to be delivered over to Whitemoor Farm the following weekend complete with tack, brushes and his winter rug. Until that time the atmosphere in the West household was electric in anticipation of his arrival. Every spare moment of that first week in May was spent talking about horses, reading about horses and dreaming about horses, so much so that when Saturday came William and Maria and particularly Emily considered themselves somewhat expert on all matters of an equine nature. It was somewhat embarrassing therefore when Rascal stubbornly refused to get off the horse box upon his arrival at Whitemoor Farm. Emily tried her hardest to coax him down the ramp but all four legs were locked in defiance. Mr Harvey had to come to the rescue in the end, unceremoniously prodding Rascal's bottom with a broom handle (a technique not described in any text book that Emily had read). But no matter, it did the trick and the rest of the weekend was spent fussing and fretting over this latest addition to the West family.

Rascal soon settled in alongside Buttons and Starlight and Emily began making real progress with an intensive course of riding lessons. William had offered lessons to Bobby as well but he was too nervous and said that for now he was happy to watch Emily and help with the grooming and feeding. Bobby loved hanging around at Whitemoor Farm. He did all sorts of little jobs that made him feel really important. He told Rascal all about school and what he did there and on a fine day he could make a game of cowboys and Indians last a good two hours. Emily too had fallen in love with Whitemoor and the time she spent there attending to Rascal's needs. Upon turning into the stable yard she would take a deep breath and close her eyes just for a second, inhaling a heady combination of the warm smell of horse hair and dung and the clear, crisp country air. Bobby would usually run off ahead and gather up their grooming kit from the tack room, whilst Emily stood absorbing the moment, still slightly giddy with the knowledge that she actually had a pony of her own.

Nearly three weeks after Rascal's arrival it was with a heavy heart that Emily had to leave him for a week whilst the West family went away for the half term holiday. For the last few years William had religiously booked up a self catering flat in a rather smart sea front block in Weston-super-Mare, but this time Maria had instigated a change. Back in January she had been reading the travel section of one of the Sunday papers and had come across an advertisement for a holiday cottage close to Woolacombe beach in Devon. It was called Tide's Reach and it sounded charming, boasting three bedrooms, a high standard 'home-from-home' interior, a large private garden and all within a short drive of the spectacular sands at Woolacombe. Maria picked up the 'phone and contacted the Mr Spencer mentioned in the advert. A lengthy and friendly conversation revealed that Tide's Reach had originally been purchased and furnished for Mr and Mrs Spencer's own use pending imminent joint retirement. Tragically, Mrs Spencer had been killed in a car crash and the dream of retiring to a beautiful cottage by the sea had been completely shattered. Mr Spencer wasn't sure if he could bear to live at Tide's Reach without his wife and had decided to rent it out for a year or two while he grieved for his loss. A good twenty minutes after first picking up the 'phone, Maria replaced the receiver, damp eyed and full of sorrow for Mr Spencer but with a confirmed booking for Tides Reach for the end of May.

When school broke up on the Friday afternoon, Emily and Bobby raced to Whitemoor Farm to say a quick goodbye to Rascal. William was champing at the bit to set off, keen to get to the Motorsafe Lodge Motel in good time for an evening meal. The plan was to stay the night here and carry on towards Devon first thing Saturday morning.

"Get off home now you two," Mr Harvey shouted across the yard. "I'll take good care of young Rascal, have no fear of that!"

"Thank you Mr Harvey," Emily called back, "We shall miss you all terribly, won't we Bobby?"

Bobby nodded his head vigorously in agreement.

"Go on with you now! And run like the wind in case your mum and dad have a mind to go without you!"

And as Mr Harvey turned to go indoors he suddenly realised that he would miss them too.

After Bobby's death, the holiday at Woolacombe took on a dream like quality, made all the more poignant due to the fact that William, Maria and Emily never went on holiday together again. William and Maria never suggested another holiday and Emily didn't like to ask. Consequently, that perfectly normal week at a perfectly normal seaside cottage called Tide's Reach became a golden time - a magical few days with memories that would last a lifetime; simple, sweet memories that became indelibly imprinted upon the minds of the three surviving members of the West family.

"Daddy," began Bobby, as he watched William traipse back and forth from the car boot to the cottage with a week's worth of food and personal belongings, "Will the tide really come right up here to the doorstep?"

"Of course not you silly head," Emily jumped in. "We're not *that* close to the beach. I bet lots of seaside cottages are called Tide's Reach when there's not even the chance of the sea reaching the bottom of the road!"

"Well, I bet after we've had lunch the ocean will be right here in the garden," said Bobby, "It may even come into the cottage and you'll have to sleep in a soggy bed."

"Not if I've pushed you into the soggy bed first you cheeky squirt!" And from the kitchen window Maria looked out and smiled as Emily chased her younger brother all around the pretty garden.

Eventually they both flung themselves down on the grass, giggling and panting. Bobby sprang up almost immediately as he saw William pull out from the car boot his new purple bucket and spade. He'd spotted some particularly colourful and shiny pebbles on the driveway and so the bucket could be put to immediate use. Emily remained sprawled out in the middle of the lawn, staring up at an almost cloudless sky, sinking her fingers between the blades of cool, lush grass. The garden was quite large and shaped in an almost perfect square, all of it laid to lawn save for a small patio area underneath the kitchen window. A wrought iron table and four chairs stood here, perfect for outdoor lunches and Maria had already remarked that perhaps they should buy a similar set of furniture for their garden when they returned home. But like any holiday, in those first few glorious hours or even first few days of escapement, the act of returning home seemed so far away it wasn't worth thinking about.

It was warm for the end of May and the forecast for the rest of the week was good. The spring weather had been kind in the south west of England and the garden at Tide's Reach was already a riot of colour; the vivid royal blue of lobelia, a carpet of solid purple from the rampant aubrietia and the harsh pinks and reds of the geraniums which were splattered around the borders at random. And in the hanging baskets were thick masses of trailing pansies, a robust plant despite its delicate appearance. Emily thought the purple and white flower heads looked rather like faces; foolish, rounded faces gazing up, unquestioning, towards the sun.

"Emily!" called Maria, pushing a large plate of sandwiches through the opened kitchen window, "Come and take these sandwiches from me and rally the troops for some lunch. If dad hasn't finishing unpacking yet tell him to take a break! If we have an early snack now we can have a full afternoon on the beach."

And for the next half hour all activity at Tide's Reach stopped as the four of them munched their way through Maria's salad and pickle sandwiches, breathing in the salty sea air, sitting around the wrought iron table in the early summer sun.

Emily hadn't seen too many beaches in her young life and Bobby even less so, but when they saw the beach at Woolacombe they soon declared it to be the most beautiful, fabulous beach in the whole world. William and Maria were inclined to agree. The sand was golden and clean, vast sheets of it stretching away in a shimmering white haze around the headland.

It was on the Tuesday, half way through the holiday when a sequence of events started that the family would later describe as 'a miracle'. In fact it made such a good story that it was told repeatedly over the years and never forgotten. The day dawned bright and clear but for once the four of them were not destined to go to the beach together. Maria hadn't seen a real shop for days (the beach hut establishment which sold ice lollies and water wings didn't count) and announced that she fancied a drive into Ilfracombe to see what the shops were 'throwing away'. The expression made William smile as in his experience the shops that Maria frequented could never be accused of throwing anything away, but rather flogging their goods at double the amount they should be! Nevertheless, a plan for the morning was made; William and Bobby would go to the beach as usual and Maria and Emily would take the car and head for the shops.

Maria had genuinely only intended to browse and absorb the holiday atmosphere of the town so it was with some surprise that she found herself and Emily entering a jewellers shop on the high street, her fingers already hovering around the zip of her purse. The foray into the shop was made all the more exciting because of its impulsive nature and both of them had to suppress the urge to giggle once inside and at the counter of the obviously expensive shop. Emily was momentarily dazzled by the glittering array of precious metals and stones around her; thick gold chains, platinum bangles, silver hooped earrings and countless rings and brooches set with rubies, emeralds, sapphires and diamonds. But a delicate, unassuming ring in the window was the reason why they had entered Mr Platt's Jewellery Emporium. Standing at the window, nose pressed against the glass, Emily had fallen in love with it instantly and in a rash moment one sometimes gets when shopping whilst on holiday, Maria suggested that Emily may like it for her birthday which was only six weeks away. Mr Platt himself reached into the window display in order to give them a close look at the ring in question, at the same time complimenting them on their good taste at having chosen one of the prettiest pieces in the shop. The ring slipped effortlessly onto the middle finger of Emily's right hand and Mr Platt declared it a perfect fit. The base of the ring consisted of a band of rose gold. Dead centre were two small emeralds set one above the other and to either side of this were two tiny diamonds, each the centre piece for two engraved stars. Some further intricate engraving work, swirling in pattern, finished off the piece, giving it a rather fanciful style not in the least bit out of place on a child's hand.

"We'll take it!" said Maria, with a voice which gave the impression that casually buying an expensive piece of jewellery for her daughter was an everyday occurrence. "And I'd be grateful if you could just let me see those silver hoops too…"

Ten minutes later they waved goodbye to Mr Platt and left his Jewellery Emporium, high with the excitement that expensive purchases invariably bring. Maria was sporting a beautiful pair of silver hooped earrings and Emily couldn't help staring down at her new ring every few seconds.

"You can keep it on until we've shown daddy and Bobby," said Maria, "Then I'll put it safe until your birthday." And thinking about their two dazzling purchases she made a mental note to knock off ten pounds when William asked her how much they had cost.

By the time they got to the beach it was lunchtime and William and Bobby had already set up camp in their usual favoured spot; a patch of golden sand which was flanked on one side by a small outcrop of rocks. It had become their own special place on the beach at Woolacombe and now, bare foot and carrying two giant ice creams each, Maria and Emily ran towards it, eager to show off their new purchases. After lunch William and Maria snoozed and read for the rest of the afternoon with an occasional stroll down to the water's edge for a cooling paddle. Emily and Bobby had been given permission to go farther down the beach than ever before, returning at the agreed time grubby and wet and covered in sand, Bobby with tales of sand worms and crab spiders, undoubtedly the relations of some terrible sea monster yet to be discovered. They even ate their evening meal on the beach that day; bags of thick cut salty chips covered with great squirts of tomato ketchup. Huge seagulls circled overhead, surfing the air as

William gazed up and marvelled at their enormous wing span. Their pitiful cries for food were more than Bobby could stand and most of his bread and butter ended up being flung into the air for them to swoop down and catch. It was almost dusk by the time they gathered up all their bits and headed off back to Tide's Reach. The last heat of the day had gone with the setting of the sun and it was a shivering foursome who made their way to the comforting warmth of the cottage.

They were barely through the front door when Emily realised with a plummeting heart that her wonderful new ring was missing. "My ring, it's gone! Oh mum, no! My beautiful ring has gone!"

"Oh, Emily, how on earth could that have happened? It was such a perfect fit. Oh, I just don't believe it! Are you sure it's not in your pocket? Did you put it in my handbag?"

The memory of exactly where the ring was came to Emily in an agonising flash and her heart ached with disappointment. *She* had lost the ring. It hadn't slipped off her finger or been stolen or anything else that would have been slightly easier to bear. *She* had left it on the picnic rug; right at the top corner where she had been sitting when Maria handed round the wet flannel so they could all go home with relatively clean hands. She had taken off the ring in order to clean her hands properly and caught up in the light-hearted banter and the rush to leave the beach before nightfall she had completely forgotten to put the new ring back on her finger. She felt herself blush as she shared the memory with the rest of the family, for however she tried to phrase her apologies she sounded careless, ungrateful, unable to be trusted with an expensive item of jewellery usually reserved for grownups. Maria was understandably upset but tried not to be too hard on Emily as she was so obviously devastated.

"Come on now, we mustn't let it spoil the holiday…" she began.

"Oh, dad!" cried Emily, "Let's get a torch and go back onto the beach now! We may find it…"

"But the tide will be right in by now love. I'm sorry…"

And so they went to bed, although Emily hardly slept at all, and when she did it was a sleep disturbed by childish dreams of treasure buried in the sand and dark tunnels leading to the den of a sea monster.

The End of Emily West

It was Bobby who turned the sorry sequence of events into a 'miracle'. The next morning they made their usual pilgrimage to the beach, once again heading for the sheltered bit of sand that had become their own. Emily was tired and still upset about the ring and suddenly wanted to be at home with Rascal. Bobby ran ahead with his bucket and spade making a perfect set of footprints in the as yet unblemished sand. The tide had indeed come in and gone out again and the expanse of beach spread out before them, as smooth and perfect as a piece of paper, waiting for a child to scribble upon it. Bobby flung himself down onto the sand and immediately leapt up again, shouting to them madly and waving his hands in the air.

"Your ring, Emy! I've found your ring!"

Emily scooped him up in her arms and spun him round and round. "You're a genius Bobby! Mum, dad, look! My baby brother is a genius!"

"But the tide," said William, "The tide covered this spot completely last night. Why on earth wasn't the ring washed away?"

It was a question which none of them could answer.

"Now put that ring on Emily, please," commanded Maria, "And never take it off again! I know I said you'd have to wait for your birthday but... well, this is nothing short of a miracle!"

Emily put the ring back on to her finger, and once again the beach at Woolacombe was a magical place.

On Friday, after breakfast, Bobby began to cry, wanting to know why they couldn't stay at Tide's Reach forever. William assured him they would come back next year and Emily sat him on her knee and began telling him of all the wonderful things that were waiting for them at home... Rascal, the kittens in the barn at Whitemoor Farm, the tree house dad may be persuaded to build in the garden and the local gymkhana which they could take Rascal to. Tide's Reach seemed to take on a gloomy air, stripped of their presence, waiting for the cleaners to come in and prepare it for the next family who fancied a week by the sea. By then there would be nothing to suggest that the West family had ever been there, had briefly made it their home; loving the time they had spent within its walls. Emily thought that when they got home it would be as if the cottage and the beach had only existed for them, had been made available purely for their enjoyment that week, a snapshot in time… and if she tried to look up Woolacombe or Ilfracombe Bay on a map those places simply wouldn't be there. She suddenly wanted to leave something at Tide's Reach, something from them that proved they had been here, that the cottage had been theirs.

"Get your felt tips and those star stickers," she hissed to Bobby, "And meet me in my bedroom!"

Bobby's tears gave way to the air of excitement Emily's command had created and he obediently did as she had asked. Shutting the bedroom door behind them, Emily beckoned Bobby over to the far corner of the room. Here she knelt down and carefully lifted up the fitted carpet. Exposing the wooden floorboards, Bobby realised what they were about to do. Emily signed her name first and then he signed his, decorating the multi coloured writing with gold and silver stars. Underneath their names Emily wrote, *'we will return'*. Over the course of her life Emily would occasionally wonder if the words were still written there, if the stars were still stuck to the boards, and would shed a tear for the fact that she had never been able to find out.

Chapter 5

WHEN THEY ARRIVED BACK AT OAKSIDE Grange on the Saturday afternoon, Emily and Bobby stayed in the house for no more than ten minutes before hot footing it down the lane to see Rascal. Any lingering sadness at leaving Tide's Reach was quickly banished as they turned into Whitemoor Farm and drank in the familiar sights and sounds. Several plump hens pecked their way around the yard and one of the tabby kittens, much bigger than Emily remembered it, darted in front of them to the safety of the barn. The clematis, which had been trained to grow in an arch around the front door of the Harvey's cottage, had been merely a mass of green foliage when they had left for Cornwall. Now it sported huge flower heads: great splashes of purple which showed up brilliantly against the white paintwork. 'Time and tide wait for no man' thought Emily. It was one of her dad's favourite phrases and given the subtle changes that had happened in just one short week it now seemed so apt. Time and tide wait for no man. Rascal was already in his stable and when he saw Emily and Bobby his ears pricked up in anticipation of treats. Mr and Mrs Harvey came out of the cottage and Mr Harvey thrust a piece of paper into Emily's hand whilst his wife scooped up Bobby and he buried his head in her ample bosom.

"Aye, it hasn't been the same in the yard without you two young 'uns running 'round the place," said Mr Harvey.

"Oh it certainly hasn't," agreed Mrs Harvey as Bobby lifted his face up for air, "But it was a treat to get your postcard – that beach looked just splendid! And then yesterday Mrs Loxley from Ferndale dropped off the schedule for the gymkhana and we knew you'd be as keen as mustard to have a look at it and see which classes Rascal can be entered for!"

Mrs Harvey rattled on about life at Whitemoor over the last week as Emily digested the details of the Ferndale Horse Show & Gymkhana. The event was split into two sections; the horse show which featured show jumping classes, 'handy pony' and 'best turned out' and then the gymkhana, where the prospect of competing for a rosette in things like the sack race and the egg and spoon race made Emily almost tremble with excitement. There was surely no time to loose - they must practice, practice, practice! And that night she lay in bed hugging her knees to her chest and wondering if she had the skill or indeed the nerve to enter Rascal in the handy pony class. He'd need to be bathed, his mane and tail plaited, his hooves polished and his saddle and bridle would have to gleam and sparkle like never before. And what on earth was *she* going to wear? Her horse books told her that horse show classes demanded a white shirt and navy tie, snowy white jodhpurs, black Jodhpur boots and a single breasted navy jacket preferably with a velvet collar. It all sounded terribly expensive and she just couldn't ask for any more to be spent on her. She touched the ring on her finger and resolved to make the best of what she already had in her wardrobe, wondering if her school blazer might just pass as a show jacket… she'd have to cover the badge up on the top pocket. This and a thousand more details which must be addressed before the Ferndale Show zipped through her mind before she finally drifted off to sleep.

Over the next five weeks Rascal was groomed and pampered and put through his paces. Mr Harvey had sectioned off a small strip of land at the top of the main field specifically for the purpose of gymkhana and handy pony practice. Bobby cheered on Emily as she galloped about with sacks and spoons and eggs that usually ended up broken. The ground was becoming hard and the grass was giving way to dust, and the country's leading weather men were predicting a blazing, glorious summer. The week before the show, during one of these practice sessions, Mr Harvey came running out to them with some news from Mrs Loxley.

"Just got off the telephone." he called, "Come on Bobby lad, it's your turn now! Mrs Loxley says there's been a right uproar 'cos there's no fancy dress class in the schedule. That'd be just grand for you Bobby – get yourself a funny costume and just sit tight in the saddle and Emily can lead you around the ring. Everyone gets a rosette in that class Mrs Loxley says so get your thinking caps on."

Bobby didn't need any further encouragement to enter the fancy dress competition and knew almost immediately what he wanted to appear as. "A horse fly, Emy, let me be a horse fly!" he pleaded and in the few days left running up to the show Maria worked diligently on Bobby's horse fly costume; a vision of glossy black satin and huge iridescent wings.

On the first Saturday in July Emily woke up to the alarm at five o'clock sharp. She tiptoed into Bobby's room and helped him to get dressed. She made toast and jam for them to wrap in napkins and take to the stables although she knew she would be unable to eat a thing until the show was over. Walking down the lane at five thirty it seemed to Emily that they may be the only two human beings in the world who were awake. In an hour or two others would rise from their beds and the noise of their clatter and movement would spill from their homes into the outside world; the bark of a dog, the clink of milk bottles, the revving of a tired car engine. All this and more would intrude upon this crisp, dewy peace that just at this moment Emily and Bobby could claim as their own. This was the moment to savour; the calm before the storm, the anticipation of winning, of looking fabulous, of envious glances from other riders and of riding home with Rascal's bridle smothered in rosettes. It was hardly even warm as yet but the air held a strong promise of heat. There was that *smell* in the atmosphere; the unmistakable smell of summer and as Emily excitedly prepared Rascal for an assault of bubbles, brushing and plaiting she told Bobby that this was going to be the best summer of their lives. *The best summer Bobby, the best summer of our lives!* How many times she would look back to that conversation and wonder if she herself hadn't tempted fate and brought about the terrible misfortune that was now only three weeks away. Had it been too much to boast about what a fantastic summer they were having, and hoped to have still? Had she angered the gods with her carefree, gleeful manner? And had they rewarded her by bringing about Bobby's downfall, bringing this magical summer to a premature and tragic end?

By the time she and Rascal arrived at the Ferndale Show Emily thought she might be sick. It had been one thing dreaming about this day but the reality of it was testing her nerve to the limit. Where she had fantasised about other riders looking at her and Rascal with envy, she was now happy to simply blend in. Where she had dreamt of returning home with fists full of rosettes, she was now happy with the thought of just one. William, Maria and Bobby had driven the two miles to the showground and were waiting for her inside the entrance. Maria had got her school blazer pressed and ready and Bobby helped with the final touches to Rascal by applying the hoof polish. They were flying through the classes and Emily soon found herself riding into the main ring for the handy pony class. The fourteen contestants were timed with a stop watch as in turn they negotiated their way around the handy pony course. It was like an assault course, with all manner of obstacles to get over, under and across in the fastest time. Emily appeared to guide Rascal around with expert precision and earned a third place for her efforts. A large yellow rosette with three satin tail ribbons adorned Rascal's bridle as they cantered out of the ring. Everyone was clapping and cheering and the spectator members of the West family found themselves grinning from ear to ear, shouting *well done* and *congratulations* whilst patting Rascal on the neck and Emily on the back. Had ever a moment been so sweet? And there was more to come. The serious business of the showing and the jumping classes gave way to the down and dirty business of the gymkhana, where arms and legs flapped away furiously in an effort to win the mad dash to the finish line. Eggs were broken, sacks were torn and knees were grazed in the undignified scramble for rosettes and William later swore to Maria that he'd never witnessed anything quite so funny. Emily came second in the egg and spoon and scooped a coveted red rosette, a first, for her part in the sack race. Her day had been perfect and she thanked

William again and again for letting them have this wonderful pony. All she had to do now was lead a rather tired looking Rascal around the ring for Bobby's fancy dress class and she felt herself glow with pride at the sight of the shiny black little creature now sitting in the saddle.

"A *horse* fly – how clever!" Was the general murmuring around the ring. There was a ballerina, a clown, an Arabian prince, a cowboy and a Red Indian, but nothing quite as inventive and ingenious as a horse fly, so inevitably Bobby also found himself to be the proud owner of a bright red rosette.

"We won, we won!" he shouted to any one who'd listen, and he pinned the rosette to his fly costume which he absolutely refused to take off until it was time for his bath. Emily and Bobby posed for pictures either side Rascal, his head drooping with rosettes and sheer tiredness and soon after that they left the showground for the slow plod home.

The following week it was Emily's birthday. She took a cake into school to share with her friends, most of who had been invited to her party – a disco to be held on the coming Saturday at the local village hall. On the afternoon of the party, whilst decorating the hall with balloons and streamers and banners, Maria and William sighed and remembered some of Emily's parties of the past; pink themed parties with fairies and magicians, face-paints and make believe. Never mind that one of the fairies had been well past the first flush of youth or that one of the magicians had been so nervous he was all fingers and thumbs. High on party games and the promise of jelly and ice-cream the children were enthralled, their innocent gaze quite oblivious to the short comings of those who performed in front of them. Last year Maria had remarked that it would probably be the last birthday Emily asked for the likes of Moonshine the Party Fairy. And she was right. This year's trend amongst Emily's peers was for village hall discos or barbeques on the back lawn with a tape deck for entertainment. Gone were the days of pass the parcel and pin on the tail on the donkey and Maria had to comfort herself with the knowledge that it would be a few years yet before Bobby's enthusiasm for musical statues and wizards gave way to flashing lights and pop music.

Emily remembered that night with perfect clarity, the memories of it made all the more vivid by virtue of being the last time they were all together, celebrating, laughing and revelling in the joy of life – having a perfect time at a perfect party. The disc jockey hired for the occasion was called Tiny Tom, although he was anything but. He was stoutly built with long mousey hair and a spotty forehead and he made Emily and her friends giggle with his 'Emily Rocks!' DJ speak. The specialist discotheque lighting was amazing and the whole evening passed in a multi-coloured whirl. The party food could hardly be identified for the array of flashing colours which illuminated the long trestle table on which it lay and William laughed that getting a plate of grub here was like taking your chances at a lucky dip. Emily also remembered that evening for being the first time that Paul Andrew had made a real point of speaking to her and making it clear that he really liked her. As a group of them danced Emily could feel his eyes upon her. She felt vaguely embarrassed and her feet suddenly became awkward and out of time with the music. She wanted to look in any direction but his, and wondered why the attentions of someone who had been a classmate for seven years should bring about this air of discomfort.

"Brilliant party, Emily!" said Paul, talking closely into her ear in order to be heard above the music and the excited chatter of Tiny Tom.

"Thanks," she replied, glad of the disco lights which masked her furious blushing.

"Someone told me you have a pony. Could I see him sometime do you think..?"

"Yes, of course! Definitely… I mean that'd be brilliant… if you'd really like to."

"Yeah, well, just let me know…"

And with a winning smile meant only for her, Paul turned to get himself a plate and pick at the array of food on offer.

Numerous birthday presents accumulated in the village hall kitchen – an area of wine, beer and sanctuary for Maria and William and several of the parents who had preferred to stay for the duration of the party. Knowing that Emily had a younger brother, many of Emily's friends (or presumably their mothers who knew how a sibling hates to be left out) had included a gift for Bobby too. Bobby had been allowed to invite one special friend to the party to keep him company and he and his friend Jamie spent much of the evening hiding under the food table munching crisps and cake and periodically checking on the state of the 'present pile'.

As the birthday girl Emily was, quite naturally, the centre of attention and she loved every rainbow coloured moment of that balmy Saturday night. *She* was holding a disco party. Paul Andrews liked her and she liked him. It made her feel cool, 'with it', a girl about town and easily confirmed her status as one of the most liked, most popular girls in her class. Nothing beat that feeling of being belle of the ball and she cursed the clock which forged ahead with its journey; restless hands which ticked and tocked, unaware that she wanted time itself to stop so she could savour the moment some more. It was less then two weeks later that she wished the clock would stop forever, not to savour any moment but to freeze them all, to suspend the whole family in time and release them from the pit of despair they'd tumbled into.

Chapter 6

THEY WERE AT WHITEMOOR FARM WITH Rascal when Bobby first mentioned that he felt unwell. It was the last day of the summer term and they had gone to Whitemoor straight from school. Mrs Harvey saw Bobby sitting on a bale of straw in the yard. Emily was mucking out the stable and it was unusual for Bobby not to be helping. She carried over a tray with some orange squash and ginger biscuits.

"Eh, you've got the right idea Bobby – it's too hot to do anything today, isn't it love?"

"It's not that I don't think," he said. "I just don't feel very well…"

"Tell me what's the matter then and in the meantime we'll see if one of my ginger biscuits won't put it right!"

Emily came out of the stable with the wheelbarrow and helped herself to the juice and biscuits.

"What's up Bobby?" she asked, hoping that he wasn't pulling a sulk because Paul was due to come over later.

"It's my head… it really hurts. My arms and legs hurt too. They ache, Emy. I've been aching all day and it's getting worse. I want to go home…" And with that he bent his head and began to cry, the uneaten ginger biscuit falling to the floor.

"Oh, you poor lamb!" said Mrs Harvey, clucking and fussing around him. "It sounds like the flu to me, and in all this heat too!

Emily love, I think you'd best get him off home… your mum might want him in bed."

"Come on then, trouble," sighed Emily. "I'll give you a piggy back. See you later Mrs Harvey… a school friend of mine is coming 'round after tea. Paul's his name if he gets here before me."

"Right you are love, and get better soon won't you Bobby?"

Bobby managed a weak smile as he clung to his sister's back and rested his throbbing head on her shoulder.

Emily trudged up the lane in the full glare of the sun, wondering if it wouldn't have been easier to wheel Bobby home in the barrow! She noticed that the white and purple foxgloves growing on the verge had started to droop through lack of rain. Once bright and ramrod straight they now leaned as if they were about to fall over and were covered in a fine layer of dust. *I know just how you feel* she thought as Bobby got heavier on her back and sweat began to run in tiny rivulets down her face.

Maria was unloading some shopping from her car as they turned into the drive.

"Bobby! What on earth's the matter?"

"He says his head hurts, mum," said Emily, "And his arms and legs too. Says he's been aching all day and now he feels worse. Mrs Harvey thinks he may have the flu."

Emily eased her grip on Bobby and let him slide off her back. But as soon as his feet touched the ground his knees buckled and he was obviously already too weak to stand. Emily, who had been intent on having a quick wash and getting back to Whitemoor to meet Paul, suddenly felt frightened at this turn of events, for it was now quite obvious that Bobby was very ill.

"Mummy's here, darling," said Maria as she scooped him up and carried him quickly into the house, "Mummy's here now, don't worry, it's going to be alright… Emily'll stay with you while Mummy calls for a doctor."

Her soothing words of calm were in sharp contrast to the rising panic that was gripping her like a vice for she knew instinctively that she should get him to the hospital. He was deathly pale and his eyes looked glazed and horribly tired, and as she lay him on the sofa he began to moan and shiver.

"Mum, what wrong with Bobby? What's wrong with him?"
"It's alright Emily, it's just a really nasty flu virus… I think we should get him to the hospital though. Stay with him will you while I call for an ambulance…"
Emily knelt down and held Bobby's hand.
"So hot, Emy," he breathed, "So hot… my neck hurts too…"
"But you feel cold Bobby," she said, taking both his hands in hers.
"Think I'll sleep for a bit…"
"OK Bobby, OK my little angel… you get some sleep. Bet the doctor will give you some yucky medicine to make you feel all nice and better…"
Bobby managed a smile and Emily's heart lurched at the sight of her little brother curled up on the sofa, small and vulnerable, waiting for someone or something to make him feel better again. Maria ran back into the sitting room with news that the ambulance was on its way. She reached into the drawer of the chiffonier and found some paper and a pen and scrawled a short note for William to read when he arrived home from work, which could be any time soon. *Emily and I are at St Joseph's with Bobby. Don't panic love! Looks like a nasty virus and wanted him to see a doctor straightaway, so called an ambulance. Can you collect us? Will be at A & E I suppose. Love, Maria. X.* She looked over to see Bobby dozing peacefully and Emily still holding his hands. Should she have called an ambulance? Would she be frowned upon, branded a time waster, dialling 999 when she could easily have popped him down to the local surgery? She felt slightly guilty now that the initial panic was over; guilty and foolish, calling the already over-stretched emergency services when she should have kept her head and called the doctor for an appointment. But he had looked so awful - so weak and ill and virtually on the point of collapse. And hadn't he said he had ached all day, and that his head hurt? Surely a little boy shouldn't get a violent headache like that? Finally, she convinced herself that she had done the right thing and began to gather some things together in case they had to wait at the hospital for any length of time. Keys, money, sweets, tissues, a picture book and more were stuffed into

The End of Emily West

her bag, and very faintly in the distance, she could just make out the wailing sound of a siren. She ran out into the driveway so she could wait by the gate for the ambulance, whilst inside Emily noticed for the first time that Bobby had a faint rash on his legs. She lifted his top only to discover more angry spots and patches and as Bobby opened his eyes and groaned, two ambulance men came swiftly into the room.

"Hello little man, what's your name? Can you hear me? My name's Keith, What's yours?"

"Bobby..."

"OK then, Bobby. We're just going to take a look at you then get you to see a doctor. Fancy a ride in the ambulance do you, son?"

"Yes, please..."

Bobby was examined whilst Maria and Emily gave an account of what had happened since he mentioned feeling unwell at Whitemoor earlier. Maria was alarmed when she saw the extent of the rash and was utterly dismayed that the ambulance men seemed to be treating the case with such concern. Surely she was a timewaster, an overly concerned mother who should be severely reprimanded for mistaking the ambulance crew for a taxi service? Surely, anything but this? But the undertone of urgency was relentless and Bobby was taken quickly to St Joseph's General Hospital, sirens blaring and with Emily and Maria by his side. The man named Keith told Maria that Bobby may well have a disease called Meningitis – an infection of the covering layers of the brain called the Meninges. It was serious. Maria visibly reeled and clung to Bobby's hand even tighter, as if in an effort to literally squeeze new life into his weakened body. He was given an injection of penicillin and as Emily watched the needle enter his pale skin she wondered how she had ever been so stupid as to think *some yucky medicine* was all that was needed to make Bobby feel OK.

"Thank God," said Maria, when St Joseph's came into view and the ambulance slowed down to stop outside the Accident and Emergency Unit. "Oh thank God, we're here. It's alright Bobby darling, we're here. The doctor will make it all better now, won't he Emily? We're here love, we're at the hospital."

Emily tried to give some suitable response, some words of agreement and encouragement, but none came. The words stuck in her throat and threatened to choke her, like a piece of food that would go neither up nor down. Bobby opened his eyes and looked towards her but his eyes looked grey and watery, devoid of brightness and colour and in a second or two the lids closed. His lips had an unnatural blue colour about them and Emily started praying to a God she had never really believed in to let no harm come to her baby brother.

With tunnel vision, never for one moment taking in their surrounding to the left or the right, Maria and Emily followed the path of Bobby's trolley. The sense of urgency seemed to have reached fever pitch, the atmosphere was charged with emotion and fear and Maria knew that at any given moment she may tear at her hair and scream out loud for someone to help her poor son.

"Bobby…" her voice cracked as suddenly a nurse blocked her way and asked her to wait in a side room for a few moments with Emily whilst the consultant doctor examined Bobby. Four plastic chairs decorated the room and Maria sat down heavily on one of them. All pretence of calm and faith had vanished. Over the next thirty minutes Maria tried to drag every little thing she had ever heard about Meningitis to the front of her mind. People with Meningitis had headaches… they hated light didn't they and had stiff necks? And hadn't she once read about a little girl who had lost both her feet and one hand to the disease? Oh, Christ Almighty the thought was unbearable and she clung on to the fact that he was at least here in hospital, in the hands of people who could make him better. She had got him here straightaway, she had got him the medical help he needed in time; she had done the right thing. Emily wondered how long he would be in hospital for, and more immediately, how long it would be before the doctors would let them see him. How long would it be before that injection made him feel better? He'd want his favourite pyjamas bringing in of course, and in a day or two maybe the colouring book he was trying to finish.

At that very moment Mr Hayes, the consultant doctor, was shaking his head in disbelief that a healthy little boy could have succumbed to Meningococcal Meningitis so rapidly, as from all accounts he had been fully coherent just a few hours previously, albeit displaying most of the classic symptoms of the disease. He could only be thankful that the little lad's suffering had been short-lived.

Mr Hayes walked into the side room. "Mrs West..?"
He looked at Maria and Maria looked at him. His face was strained and his eyes were full of such pity and sorrow. Furthermore the atmosphere of urgency that had been felt so keenly up until now had suddenly disappeared. The race they had been so desperate to win was over and now they had to face the bitter reality of defeat.
"Oh please God, no…" Maria let out a strangled cry.
"I'm so very sorry… I can assure you we did everything we could to try and save him…"
"Noooo!" The threatened scream of anguish erupted now, as heartbreaking as the cry of a wounded animal caught in a trap. Maria gripped her hair at the roots with one hand and clawed at her cheek with the other, whilst Emily wrapped both her arms around her and closed her eyes to a world she never wanted to see again.

William entered the room then, looking dishevelled and hot, and with fear in his heart he stood still for a moment to take in the scene of devastation. He looked at Mr Hayes.
"My son, Bobby… my son…" And then he braced himself and looked at Maria.
A swollen, blotched face stared back at him and with a shake of her head that would haunt him for the rest of his days, he knew that Bobby had gone. The West family clung to each other then, Maria and William battered and broken and Emily - the thread which was just about holding them together. The sobs and cries of her parents became a muffled and distant echo as Emily tried, and failed, to take in the magnitude of what had occurred. Her parents' distraught state had shocked her to the core and it seemed to be of the utmost importance that she give whatever strength she had to keep them from simply melting away before her eyes. Random, detached thoughts ran through her head as Mr Hayes tried to explain what had happened in those final moments… her cassette deck needed new batteries… there was some old pineapple juice in a glass beside her bed… and she wondered if

Paul Andrew was still waiting for her at Whitemoor Farm, or if he had gone home – annoyed at waiting so long for her to return.

The day of Bobby's funeral dawned fine and clear as no day of any funeral has a right to. Emily remembered it mainly for two things; the coffin, which was pitifully and ridiculously small, and her mum's red and puffy, tear-streaked face – so swollen from crying that she looked like a caricature of her former self. She remembered little of the service itself or indeed the burial save for some blurred images of grief-stricken mourners and the surreal sight of the coffin being lowered into the ground. It was easier to think of other things; Rascal, school, pop music, new hair styles – anything that would take her away from St Matthew's church and its graveyard. But invariably her random thoughts would ultimately take her back to Bobby – his favourite training shoes, a lost tooth, the unfinished colouring book… and the memory of him sitting on the bale of straw outside the stable, aching and crying, his ginger biscuit falling to the floor.

Emily woke up with a start under the sycamore tree and checking her watch found that she'd been asleep for over an hour.
Time and tide wait for no man.
Mr or Mrs Harvey must have been to check on her because a tumbler full of orange squash sat beside her, covered over with a paper napkin to protect the sweet juice from the summer flies. She drank it all thirstily before catching Rascal and walking him up to the yard. He still had to be brushed. He still had to be brushed and ridden and taken to shows and loved. Mrs Harvey brought out more juice when she had finished and she flopped down on the cobbles, exhausted but satisfied with her work. It was tea time and the heat of the day had given way to a more pleasurable and bearable warmth. Released from his head collar, Rascal ambled back down the field to join the other ponies. A persistent and angry wasp tried in vain to taste some of the remaining orange juice… one of the farm cats rolled over on its back, enjoying the summer sun without a care in the world, and looking up Emily

saw several thick ribbons of aeroplane smoke criss-crossing in the sky. It was time to walk home; out of the yard and down the lane and into the gravelled driveway of Oakside Grange. But Oakside had changed; the dull and dismal air of their recent loss found its way into every room, worked its way into every nook and cranny. Bobby's presence was felt in every brick, in every piece of furniture, in every stick and stone as the poor house and its dwellers silently screamed out for him to be returned.

As Emily left the stables to go home, it seemed to her that the journey had never before been so long and arduous.

Chapter 7

ON THE DAY OF BOBBY NORTH'S funeral, twenty four year old Darren O'Dowel was floating around Blackpool sea front, spaced out of his head on LSD. His old university pal, Michael Sheldon was getting married in a week's time and had chosen Blackpool as the venue for his stag party. That riotous night had been a few days ago and whilst Michael and his conscience had scuttled back over to Manchester to be with his future bride, Darren, John and Barry had chosen to bum around the bright lights of the north west's most famous seaside town a little longer. At six o'clock that morning, following another night lost to the effects of cocaine, cannabis and cheap whiskey, each of the three placed a tab of acid under his tongue, kissing goodbye to reality for at least another twenty four hours. At seven o'clock, ignoring Mrs Holby's offer of a 'nice fry up for breakfast', all three staggered out of The Holby Bed & Breakfast and headed for the front. The LSD had started to work its magic. Nothing mattered but this moment in time and the world around them had taken on a unique and vibrant air. The sea had never crashed so loudly, had never before produced a foam that was so dazzlingly white. The buildings, the roads, the trams, which yesterday had looked rather flat and dull now looked vividly three dimensional and hugely entertaining. Life in general had never held so much promise. This was the high, the fun part of the LSD experience and Darren for one was anticipating its full effect with a great deal of greed

The End of Emily West

and relish. Drink and drugs, drugs and drink; the ultimate escape. He started to giggle... a quiet titter at first which rapidly developed into an uncontrollable fit of laughter that had him doubled over on the pavement. He'd imagined that one of the oncoming trams had winked at him and it was the funniest, most hilarious, priceless thing that had ever happened to him in his entire life. John and Barry's senses were also working overtime and within minutes all three of them were sitting on the pavement, aching all over from the strain of such strenuous laughter. Totally oblivious to the bizarre sight the three of them made, they staggered up to some railings and gripped on to them for dear life, eyes streaming tears and noses dripping mucus as they continued to find humour in things that the sober eye wouldn't give the time of day. The roller coaster continued and all three of them were exhausted from the strain of riding on it; dizzy and breathless yet desperate for the next thing that would trigger another round of ridiculous high-pitched cackling and escapism.

It took them nearly two hours to make the journey from the promenade to the beach below. Five paces and fifteen stone steps had never been quite so difficult to conquer. They sat down in the sand and gazed, unseeing, out to the ocean. They sat in silence; the laughter phase of the trip was well and truly over. Barry picked up some wet sand and watched, fascinated, as sticky chunks of it slid through his fingers. The loose grains, the sensation of them slipping and moving... the harshness, the beauty... for the next hour and a half he looked at nothing but the golden mush in his hands and wondered why he'd never before realised that the meaning of the universe lay in great big handfuls of Blackpool sand.

John looked at his shoelaces and started to cry. He'd never seen shoelaces before that looked quite so forlorn. These laces weren't just old and tired and grubby... they were *suffering*. They were limp and useless. They'd given up on any meaningful kind of existence because John hadn't looked after them properly. They were shrivelling to nothing before his eyes. The laces squirmed and wriggled in their last dying moments and then in one final act of defiance swelled to ten times their normal size, hissing and spitting in his face before withering away to nothing.

"Jesus, oh sweet Jesus!" John covered his face and wept even louder, pushing his knuckles into his eyes to obliterate the memory. The laces in Darren and Barry's shoes must be angry now. He'd let them down, failed them. All the shoelaces of the world would unite and come after him, track him down, slither their way around his neck, wrap themselves around his throat, tighter and tighter until the last breath had been squeezed from his body.

Must get away from shoelaces.

"Jesus Christ, Jesus *Christ*!" John jumped up and tore the shoes from his feet before lurching clumsily towards the steps that would lead him back up on to the prom.

The others barely noticed his departure and furthermore they didn't really care. Barry was still totally absorbed in the sand and Darren wasn't even on the beach anymore. His physical form lay horizontal on Blackpool sands but his mind was journeying towards a different world. He approached the cage. A clown… a real clown crying real tears stood beside it and bade him to come closer. "We've got him, Darren," whispered the clown, "We've got him here for you… it's very sad… I'm so very sad… Darren, my friend, can you bear to look?"

Darren nodded dumbly then lowered his eyes. He hadn't expected it to be anyone else. "Father…"

And his father stared back at him with a look of hatred that brought Darren to his knees.

Darren O'Dowel was born on a wet and windy November night in Cambridge. His parents, Albert and Elsa, hadn't been getting on for some time and Elsa had made the classic mistake of imagining that a baby would miraculously put their rocky relationship on a firmer footing. It didn't. For each of their sakes they should have cut their losses and divorced whilst they were still childless, but Elsa had begged and pleaded and finally persuaded Albert that a bonny little baby would be their salvation. With Darren's birth Elsa's dreams of a perfect, loving, rosy family life quickly gave way to the harsh reality of chronic fatigue,

The End of Emily West

smelly nappies, throbbing breasts and a foul tempered husband. She woke up one morning and decided she'd had enough. She packed a bag for herself and Darren and two hours later arrived on her mother's doorstep.

"Don't you go thinking you can just shrug off marriage like an overcoat my girl!" was all the welcome she got and so she turned around quickly and headed home, tail between her legs and resigned to her lot in life as a downtrodden, resentful mother and a very bitter wife. She had left her husband and returned to him in the space of just a few hours, and as Albert had spent the day chained to his desk he had absolutely no idea of his wife's brief desertion. Not that he would have been entirely bothered if he had have known. Albert was far too preoccupied in trying to carve out a suitable career for himself, befitting his superior intellect, than to be worried about whether Elsa and Darren went or stayed.

He had graduated from Cambridge a few years earlier with a degree in English but somehow had never got the breaks he thought were due to him – a source of acute annoyance usually taken out on Elsa. What Albert failed to realise was that he was completely deluding himself as far as his intellectual prowess was concerned. He was so quick to be a snob, so quick to sneer at others, so quick to intimidate those around him, so quick to show off. He thought he was supremely clever, based only on a firm belief that everyone around him was either backward, unambitious or downright thick. He'd left a series of promising jobs in private industry due to his inability to be a team player and now he'd swapped an office desk for a school one, treating senior school students to his vast range of knowledge and wisdom. He'd made a good start. He'd already identified three teachers who appeared to be weak-headed wimps with less than perfect academic credentials. God Almighty, he'd be head of the English Department before these buffoons who called themselves teachers could blink and then he might set his sights towards that rather lucrative head master's position. God only knew how the crusty old half-brain who was there at the moment had talked his way into *that* top job. And so once again Albert embarked upon a path of snobbery and back-stabbing that would get him absolutely nowhere.

Having a young son did nothing to mellow Albert O'Dowel. Throughout Darren's toddler years Albert's career did not make the progress he had so arrogantly assumed it would and he stayed very much on the bottom rungs of the teaching ladder. He was really not interested in Darren or his development and knew that he wouldn't be until the child started to talk properly and had the ability to hold a decent conversation. Until that point he simply wasn't worth Albert's precious time and energy. Strangely enough Darren hardly faired much better with his mother. Elsa's original plan had failed; a baby had not helped her marriage one little bit, only made it worse. Albert had immersed himself into his work and was finding comfort in beer and scotch instead of her. Darren's very presence seemed to annoy him and Elsa seriously began to wish he had never been born. She knew it wasn't natural for a mother to have these feelings but nevertheless this was the conclusion she had come to. Due to a small but more than adequate inheritance she hadn't done a day's work in her life and had no intention of ever doing so. The days were hers to do with as she pleased. Consequently Darren had become a serious burden, needing constant attention and entertainment when Elsa should have been out shopping, playing tennis or having lunch with friends. Sometimes she would leave him alone in the house with nothing more than a picture book and some paper and crayons for company whilst she nipped into town to sift through the latest clothes and cosmetics. At first she was racked with guilt but after a while they both got used to the arrangement and in the end it seemed quite normal. Elsa comforted herself with the thought that Darren would soon be starting school and would be out of her hair for a good proportion of the day. Darren comforted himself in quite a different way…

It was during the summer before he started school that Elsa started leaving him in the house on his own on a regular basis. Darren was a naturally bright little boy and big for his age, and so got very practised in fending for himself when he had to. Due to his mother's absence, both physically and mentally, and his father's total indifference he had become very much a loner. He had little idea of how to play with other children and was seriously lacking in matters of social etiquette – something he would pay for dearly when he started school.

If Elsa thought that Darren spent all his time alone simply looking at picture books and making colourful patterns on pieces of paper she was very much mistaken. He took delight in revenge. Childish things of course but acts of revenge even so. He never, ever used the bathroom in the house when he was on his own. His mother took some pride in their small, neat rear garden and so it made a perfect target. The plants and flowers got her love and attention and must therefore be punished. When the urge took him Darren liked nothing more than to pee all over her favourite blooms. When he released his yellow stream onto those silly flower heads he imagined his mother's silly face looking on in horror. He often laughed at the image. One day whilst he was peeing on some yellow pansies he laughed so long and loud that a neighbour came out of their house and looked over the fence. Darren turned around and grinned at her, then stuck his tongue out and said 'piss off' – one of his father's favourite phrases. The neighbour marched back inside with a 'well I *never*' and wondered how a little boy had learnt to be quite so rude. If Darren needed to do a poo he did it on the grass, then later sniggered as he watched his mother carefully pick it up with pieces of tissue, all the time cursing the neighbourhood dogs and their irresponsible owners. And Darren developed a fascination for insects. Dead ones worked for his purposes but if he found them alive he would soon see to it that the life was quickly snuffed out of them. A spider or fly or small moth could so easily be crushed under a spoon and mixed with the instant coffee in the jar – a hot drink that both his parents enjoyed in the morning. And for the rest of the time he would just make mischief; hide his mother's favourite pot of night cream, bend the nib of his father's fountain pen, sprinkle a little salt into the sugar bowel, spit into the milk which he then avoided drinking.

When he at last started school he had a rude awakening. Saying 'piss off' earned him a painful canning from the head teacher. Stamping on spiders in the playground or pulling the wing off a moth lost him potential friends and his dark brooding eyes and angry manner invariably meant he was on his own, always on the outside looking in, always wanting to join in but never knowing how. None of the teachers really took a shine to him although he showed himself to be bright and a fast learner. He was a very capable boy but not a pleasure to teach. As the next few years of his primary school education went by he became a disruptive influence in class, but always succeeded in being so in a very subtle manner. He would goad weaker class mates into doing things they knew they shouldn't and he would drive teachers mad by asking them a series of ridiculous or awkward questions. One newly qualified teacher found herself in tears in the staff room at break time, his tireless, endless questions about dead bodies and decaying corpses had diverted her attention from the rest of the class and the ensuing chaos had been difficult for a novice such as herself to cope with. Not one teacher found him in the least bit endearing, although all admitted he would probably leave school with an above average academic record.

He was nine years old when his father started to show some interest in him. Darren knew that his father was so brainy, so clever, so superior to others that he was desperate to win his approval. His father didn't suffer fools. His father didn't have time for dead-weight, lazy friends. His father told things as they were and if he didn't agree with something he made sure everyone knew about it. These were the things therefore which Darren aspired to, the characteristics he tried to mirror, the standards he lived by. And like a whipped dog will still try to gain his master's approval, so it was with Albert and his son. One evening when Darren had just finished a writing assignment for his English homework, Albert walked into the kitchen and looked at the project over Darren's shoulder.

"The phrase you've used in the first line of the last paragraph is tautological," he said.

"What does tautological mean?" asked Darren

"I can't believe you don't know," replied Albert and slowly tore the three pages of work into shreds not two inches from Darren's face. "But perhaps now you'll be bothered to find out."

Darren found out its meaning the very next day and proceeded to laugh and sneer at others who were thick enough to make tautological errors in their work.

Darren was twelve when he found out that his mother had a lover – something she had managed to keep from her son and husband for the last six years. She hadn't kept the same lover in that time but had got though a string of men friends – some for money, some for sex and some for a rather satisfying combination of the two. Her current beau was a gentleman called Jeremy Lloyd, the husband of a well-to-do neighbour who had started to host cheese and wine evenings for 'a select few'. Albert hated such frivolous social situations full of twittering women and hen pecked men and refused to be Elsa's escort. Thus she went along on her own and quickly caught the eye of her host's husband – the dashing Mr Lloyd, a charismatic salesman for an electrical engineering company. He was everything that Albert wasn't; fun-loving, happy-go-lucky, carefree, sexy, adventurous, tanned, tonned and open to offers. Elsa spied her opportunity and offered herself on a plate.

"All on your own, my dear?" asked Jeremy as he topped up Elsa's glass with a particularly crisp Chardonnay.

"Yes," replied Elsa, already flattered by the attention of such a handsome looking chap. "I'm afraid cheese and wine evenings aren't quite my husband's cup of tea."

"Oh dear, perhaps we could rustle him up some coffee and biscuits!" quipped Jeremy.

"Ha! More like a stiff scotch and a copy of The Times!"

Already the two of them had formed an alliance; within seconds of meeting they were already betraying Albert, having a laugh at his expense.

"Well that's just too bad, leaving the social butterfly to fly around on her own…"

"Oh, I'm rather used to making my own entertainment, Mr Lloyd…"

"Jeremy, please."

"… My husband is a teacher and that means long days at school followed by long nights marking his students' work."

"You must get very lonely, Mrs…"

"Elsa, Elsa O'Dowel."

"You must get very lonely, Elsa." His green eyes bored into hers.

"Oh, I certainly do. But as I said, I am rather good at making my own entertainment. What's the use of living if one can't have a little fun?"

"Indeed! Couldn't agree more... but does Mr O'Dowel quite approve of you creating your own... amusement?"

"Well it would be unfair, surely, to burden him with all the details." Elsa drained her glass and Jeremy re-filled it.

"Oh yes, terribly unfair... I say, if you're taken with this Chardonnay I can always get hold of it for you. A jolly good friend of mine happens to be a wine merchant..."

"How kind of you. Does he deliver?"

"No... but I do."

And so the seed was sown and the arrangement was made - wine delivered to the house by Jeremy himself for payment in kind. And Elsa always gave good value. In fact one day she was so busy upstairs thanking Jeremy for two bottles of Chateau Rausan-Segla that she completely lost track of the time and didn't hear Darren enter the house by the kitchen door.

Darren threw down his school bag on the kitchen floor and headed upstairs to his room. Half way up he paused, gripping the hand rail until his knuckles turned white. He could hear noises coming from his parents' bedroom. What was his father doing home at this time? He strained to hear and soon realised that the male voice was not that of his fathers'. A shriek of laughter, a grunt, a groan, a slap, more laughter. Darren went to the bedroom door and slowly, quietly, turned the handle. His naked mother was on all fours, her pale creamy bottom had red slap marks all over it. Her breasts hung down like great pink udders and Darren stood and watched as a man he didn't recognise, who was also completely naked, thrust his thing in between her bottom cheeks.

"Oh dear Christ, give it to me Jeremy, give it all to me now!"

Jeremy.... Darren closed the door softly and left the house.

Darren sat on a wall at the end of the road and debated long and hard as to exactly how he was going to break the news to his father. He wasn't upset and he wasn't angry, in fact he was weighing up all his options with a huge amount of glee and satisfaction. His father would be humiliated and shamed to the very core of his being and would surely unleash a fury on his mother that would have her trembling with fear and begging for mercy. He smiled to himself as he remembered the days, long ago, when he had tried to punish her for leaving him alone by peeing on her favourite flowers. He'd just been playing. His father would show her what *real* punishment felt like. Of that he had no doubt.

It was almost a week later before the perfect opportunity arose to reveal to his father what his mother had been up to. Elsa came downstairs at seven o'clock, dressed up and ready to walk down the road to Margaret Lloyd's cheese and wine evening.

"God!" began Albert, "Doesn't that woman have anything better to do than swan about arranging cheese and wine parties? I'll bet she doesn't know one bottle of cheap plonk from the other. Bumped into the husband the other day. Typical shallow salesman... what's his name?"

"Jeremy..."

"Yes, Jeremy, that's right. God, I've got some marking to wade through tonight I can tell you..."

Darren piped up to his mother, "Is that the same Jeremy who comes around here some days?"

Elsa stared back at him with fear in her eyes. She composed herself quickly.

"Around here? Of course not, Darren. I really have no idea what you mean."

Albert put down his pen, his senses suddenly on full alert.

"What makes you think that man has been in this house?"

"Because I've seen him here... only last week in fact. You remember don't you mother?" He gazed up at his mother with a sweet innocence that made her want to reach out and slap his face.

"Is this right, Elsa?" asked Albert.

"Oh, silly me! Yes, of course... he popped around to remind me about the cheese and wine party this evening... Margaret sent him."

Albert continued to stare at his wife.

Darren said, "But why did she send him round without his clothes on?"

For a moment time itself seemed to stand still. The clock in the hallway noisily ticked away the seconds and some children could be heard laughing and playing in a neighbouring garden. A bird fluttered onto the window ledge and just as quickly flew away. A stray tabby cat chased a leaf across the garden. Life went on everywhere apart from in the O'Dowel family kitchen.

"Really, Darren!" Elsa was flushed and teary eyed. "I simply can't think why you would say such a…"

"Shut up!"

"But Albert, darling, Darren is really saying the most silly…"

"I said, *shut up*!" and he sprang up and slapped his wife across the face with such force she fell to the floor.

Darren looked down at his mother then looked across to his father. "Sorry," he said, the wide-eyed innocent boy again, "But I'm only saying what I saw the other day up in your bedroom. I mean, it's wrong to tell lies, isn't it, or keep bad secrets? That's what they teach us at school anyway." And calmly, coolly, he left the kitchen and crept up to his room. His job was done.

"Come and sit down, Elsa," said Albert. His tone was almost friendly. "Sit down here and tell me all about it. Try not to leave anything out now will you? I've sometimes wondered how you manage to fill your days, and now you're going to enlighten me."

Elsa was scared to tell the truth and just as scared not to and as Darren had envisaged she ended up on her knees begging for forgiveness. Her confession was over and she pleaded with Albert to believe her when she promised to be a faithful and dutiful wife from this day on. Albert continued to stare at her. Make-up was streaked down her face and her eyes were half closed with puffiness. A bruise had formed on her left cheek where Albert had struck her.

"You little slut," he said darkly, the words coming out thick and almost slurred with fury. "You disgusting little *whore*. Fucking for a bottle of wine! And what did you do for him if he turned up with a vintage year? How far did you go then?"

"It wasn't like that…" wailed Elsa.

"Then why don't you show me what it *was* like? I've got a decent bottle of red somewhere…"

Elsa stared after him in disbelief.

"Ah yes, here it is. Should get a decent performance out of you for this."

The cork popped out. Albert gripped the bottle in one hand and his wife's hair in the other.

"Get upstairs."

Albert pushed Elsa violently onto the bed, pulling out great clumps of her hair in the process. He forced every drop of the wine down her throat before forcing the empty bottle between her legs. When he was eventually satisfied he'd done enough with the bottle he rammed himself into her mouth and asked her repeatedly if she had now learnt her lesson. Elsa could do nothing but nod.

Chapter 8

IF THE SCHOOL SUMMER HOLIDAYS OF 1976 started out on a tragic, disastrous note, they did (at least for Emily) get slightly better. Children, by their very nature, treat death in a totally different way to adults and so it was not difficult for Paul Andrew and Karen Black to come bounding over to visit Emily that summer, offering hope and happiness in a way that only the young know how. Karen was Emily's 'best friend'. Adults have groups of friends, a circle of friends, close friends and acquaintances, whereas most children have a definite 'best friend'. As children we are utterly convinced that these friends will be in our lives forever, the partnership seemingly unbreakable. Karen and Emily were going to go to college together, get a flat together, get jobs together and could never have dreamt for one moment that there would come a time when it was hard to remember what each other looked like; a vague recollection of the other's image would remain, but the sharp clarity of the facial features, all the details they knew so well, would completely disappear. Both Paul and Karen had attended Bobby's funeral, accompanied by their respective parents and both had made a point of trying to catch Emily's eye with the hope of offering some support. Emily registered their presence and was grateful – even more so when they turned up at Whitemoor over a week later with smiles, a cassette deck and a picnic.

Paul Andrew was what parents would describe as a 'nice lad'. He had a cheerful grin, wore clean clothes and was polite to his elders. Maria and William knew of him and William for one certainly liked him, not minding in the least that he chose to keep company with Emily. He was a 'nice lad' who came from a respectable family – it was just a shame, thought William, that his spotty, sulky, teenage years were just around the corner.

"I'm glad Paul and Karen are seeing so much of Emily," William ventured to Maria one evening. "They're doing her a power of good."

"Yes, they're nice kids…"

Maria felt the familiar sting of tears and she reached for a tissue in an effort to wipe them away before they had a chance to really flow.

"Oh, love…" William put his arms around her.

"Christ Will, I almost *resent* the fact she has friends who'll rally round and get her to talk and laugh. I'm almost *jealous* for God's sake. It's pathetic. But where are my friends? Oh, I know that's unfair because Julie comes round and Fiona 'phones and everyone's trying to be kind but it's all so awful. We sit and mope or talk about silly, unimportant things just to avoid talking about Bobby. And Emily skips off down the road to see Rascal and Paul and Karen and I'm sitting here thinking I shall never, ever smile or be happy again. Why Bobby, William, why? Why our baby?"

Why, why, why – the words screamed just as loudly in William's head as Maria's and that dreaded moment descended on them yet again, that moment of utter disbelief that their little boy was dead and they would never see him again; that moment of wanting to scream out to the world, *why were we chosen for this torture? Why us?*

"Emily's just dealing with it all the best way she can, love," said William softly when Maria's sobs had lessened. "And we've got to let her get on with things and be a normal little girl… but God knows she's missing Bobby as much as we are. We've just all got to stick together and help each other through this…"

Yes, *through* it, thought William, as he finished the sentence. *Through* it had certainly been the right phrase to use because there wasn't a cat in hell's chance of getting *over* it. For as long as they breathed they would never get *over* it. How thoroughly depressing he thought, that all they could ever hope to do, for the rest of their lives, was to get through this dreadful period of raw pain and settle back down in a state of numb acceptance. By Christ, he'd never seen his life panning out like this. Thank God for Emily… thank God for his beautiful little girl, because if they hadn't got her he doubted very much whether he would have the will to carry on living.

"Emily says there's a horse show up at Bagleigh this Sunday, love. We can meet her up there, take a picnic…"

"No!" Maria almost shouted out the word.

"What do you…"

"No, William, no, I just can't… I can't! The last time we did that Bobby was there too… he was a horse fly, remember? He won a rosette… he won a red rosette …"

Maria rocked back and forth in William's arms with pictures of Bobby and his iridescent wings and red rosette dancing in front of her eyes.

William kissed the top of her head and whispered softly, "We've got to try, love… for Emily, we've got to try…."

There was a knock at the door.

"Don't worry, I'll go," said William as he gave Maria's hand a tight squeeze. He caught his reflection in the hall mirror as he reached out to open the front door. "God, I look old," he muttered to himself.

"William, hello my dear. I do hope you don't mind me just turning up like this… it's just I felt I had to come and say how sorry I am…" The words came tumbling out and William was dismayed to see that Mrs Ellery's bottom lip had started to tremble.

"Oh Mrs Ellery, do come in," he said, and she followed him inside the house and into the front room.

"Maria! I do so hope I'm not intruding…"

"Oh, Mrs Ellery, how lovely to see you."

"Bobby was in Miss Butterson's class of course, not mine more's the pity, but obviously I saw him a great deal in the playground and I was always so very fond of Emily as you know… I did attend the funeral… such a beautiful service… but well, it's been praying on my mind that I didn't get chance to tell you personally how very sorry I am and that I'm thinking of you all at this dreadful time…"

The End of Emily West

More words, more regrets, more sadness came tumbling out whilst William removed himself to the kitchen to put on the kettle.

"Oh, Mrs Ellery, I'm so grateful to you for coming round. You're very brave you know... I can't tell you how many people will cross the road to avoid meeting me and having to talk about Bobby. Well lucky them, eh? They can be cowards and look the other way and trot off home to their own happy, healthy children... but I have to live with it. I have to bloody well live with it and I don't know how much longer I can do it. It's unbearable, so absolutely unbearable..."

Maria covered her face with her hands but Mrs Ellery was already by her side, rocking her in her arms. Mrs Ellery; soft, kind, dependable old Mrs Ellery. If only every school in the world had a Mrs Ellery in it thought William as he arrived back with a tray of tea and biscuits. For the next hour they talked and cried and shook their heads at the injustice of it all. The God they had all believed in for so long was testing them to breaking point and Mrs Ellery could see the last shreds of her faith being scattered to the winds. Eventually, as Mrs Ellery fussed around with her bag and coat, preparing to leave, she said, "You're actually the first people I've told but I shan't be coming back to school next term. I'm going to telephone the head teacher tonight to explain..."

Maria and William spoke in unison, "But why?"

"I'm getting too old, too weary... too close to the children... too hurt..."

"Is Bobby the reason you're leaving?" William asked gently.

"Yes, in part if the truth be told. Bobby and... Christopher... you remember him? I'm not sure if I ever quite recovered from that."

William and Maria nodded. Christopher May - the little boy who never came home.

"I want to protect them all you see, but I can't. It's a burden I've put on myself and I need to take some time off to try and make sense of it all. Maybe just this next year. Can you understand?"

Oh yes, William and Maria understood alright, although William feared that if given all the time in the world Mrs Ellery would never be able to make sense of it all. And as he waved her goodbye and wished her well, he wondered if she would ever return to the teaching profession she had once loved so much. Another life changed forever by the death of their beloved son.

Chapter 9

THE BAGLEIGH HORSE SHOW BROUGHT IT home to Emily that she and her parents were destined to deal with Bobby's death in very different ways. The resilience of youth gave Emily the ability to block out the memory of Bobby almost completely when it suited her. At any given time she could wrap herself up in her own little world and successfully shut out the misery which always lay in wait on the outside. The Bagleigh Horse Show was one such occasion when Emily climbed into her cocoon and found it hard to understand why her parents couldn't just come on in and snuggle up alongside her.

Emily burst into the house on the Friday evening carrying with her the pungent smell of stables and a holdall full of brushes ready for cleaning.

"Gosh, what a whiff," said Maria, "Do you think you can wash yourself as well as those brushes?!"

"Yes, yes," Emily replied impatiently, "But listen, great news! Mr Harvey knows someone else who's going to Bagleigh on Sunday and they've got space in their horse box for us! Isn't that brilliant? No need to hack over there wearing out poor Rascal before he's started! You can come in the box too or drive over in the car and meet me there… A *horse box* – can you believe it? What do you think?"

The End of Emily West

Her hazel eyes were bright and shining and her cheeks slightly flushed with the effort of running the last hundred yards to the house. She looked in turn at her mum and dad, so super confident of a positive reaction. In the ensuing few seconds of awkward silence her heart felt like it had plummeted to the bottom of her stomach. This wasn't meant to be happening.

"What's wrong? Dad..? What have I said..?"

"Well you see, love… I mean to say… well, I suppose we just thought you'd be going to the show on your own this Sunday…" William felt more wretched with each word that came out of his mouth. He was being a coward. He was letting her down.

"But why?" Emily frowned and looked at them both with a sense of utter confusion. "Why on *earth* would I go to the horse show on my own? You both came to the last one!"

"Well I suppose that's the point really, love. We were *all* at the last one weren't we…? I mean Bobby as well… so your mum just thinks that maybe…"

Maria sprang with such ferocity that Emily visibly flinched. "Don't you *dare* put this on to me, William!"

"But Maria, you're the one who said you couldn't face going to the show… be fair!"

"Fair? *Fair?*! Don't you two start telling me what's *fair!*" Wild eyes sparkling with tears looked at William and Emily with such pain and anger that Emily felt compelled to turn away.

"Maria, just calm down… Emily hasn't done anything wrong."

"No, but she hasn't *thought* has she? Hasn't *thought* that I may not want to go to the blasted horse show? Hasn't *thought* of the memories it'll bring back or the pain it'll cause? Bobby was with us before wasn't he? And now you both expect me to go and face that bloody show with its bloody stupid gymkhana and fancy dress classes as if nothing's happened!"

A small voice, "Mum…"

"Well something *has* happened! Bobby won't be taking part in any of it because he's *dead*! So you tell me – why would I *possibly* want to go to the Bagleigh Show on Sunday?" Her eyes were unfocused now, unseeing as she stumbled out of the kitchen and up the stairs.

"You could come for me," whispered Emily, before shouting up the stairs with a passion and anger that William had never seen before in his little girl, "*You could come for me!*"

Much later that evening Emily was lying on her bed staring up at the ceiling when Maria tapped on the door and let herself in. Maria's face was almost red raw with the effects of crying and her tangled, matted hair lay in a limp ponytail down her back. She was clutching a sodden handkerchief – a now familiar prop which she pulled and twisted at constantly and Emily noticed that she was wearing the same clothes that she'd had on the day before. She still felt angry at her and sorry for her all in the same instant and battled with herself as to which emotion would come to the fore first.

"Emily... I'm so sorry..."

Nothing can be worse for a mother than losing her child. Thoughts of that time at the graveyard, kneeling beside Bobby's final resting place, flashed though Emily's mind.

"I'm sorry too, mum."

"I just can't face a lot of things at the moment, love."

"I know... honestly."

"You shouldn't really go to that horse show on your own though..."

"It's OK. Karen and Paul may like to meet me there. They've never been to a horse show before."

"Perhaps you could give this one a miss and the three of us could go for a picnic or something... do something nice?"

Please don't make me choose.

"Well... it's just that we've been practising for it, mum. I've been looking forward to it."

Maria's voice tightened, her spine stiffened. "It's up to you of course."

Maria got up from the bed. The wet handkerchief was still being forcibly manipulated into all kinds of elaborate twists and turns.

"I'll leave it up to you then."

Emily gazed up at the ceiling again and heard the click of the door closing.

I'm going to the horse show. I'm going, I'm going, I'm going. It's not my fault Bobby died.

The decision to go to the horse show instead of on a family picnic had been surprisingly easy to make. But it was a long time before she fell asleep.

As fate would have it the decision to go or not to go was made for Emily the next day and there wasn't a thing she could do about it. A visit to Whitemoor Farm first thing the following morning found Rascal lame and looking rather sorry for himself. The local equine vet was called out and after a lot of poking and prodding diagnosed a light sprain of the nearside fetlock. He prescribed a short course of anti-inflammatory drugs and insisted that Rascal have complete rest for at least a week.

So Maria's family picnic was on. She commiserated with Emily about Rascal's lameness to which Emily mumbled, "I suppose you're happy now."

"*What* did you say?" snapped Maria, grabbing Emily roughly by the shoulder.

"I said, I suppose you're happy now…" replied Emily, jutting out her chin and trying to look Maria straight in the eye.

"How *dare* you, you nasty little girl! How *dare* you assume that I'll ever be happy again?" And Maria pushed past her into the hallway, grabbing the car keys from the sideboard and slamming the front door behind her.

William ran into the hall. "What on earth's going on?"

Emily burst in tears, "Mum called me nasty… she called me nasty…"

"Come on now, love… she didn't mean it. It's difficult for us all at the moment, isn't it?"

Emily nodded dumbly, letting her tears form a large damp patch on William's shirt. Why couldn't *they* stop thinking about Bobby in the same way that *she'd* stopped thinking about him. You could block out so much pain if you really put your mind to it, if you really hardened yourself… if you just stopped caring for a while.

"Did mum say where she was going, love?" asked William, trying not to panic at the thought of a tearful Maria driving at speed around the country lanes.

"No... she just went..."

"Well maybe she just wants to be on her own for a while. Come on, love... come and help me in the garden..."

Maria spun her car around on the gravel outside the house and sped out of the driveway with barely a glance to the left or right. The back nearside wheel slammed into the curb as she fought to bring the car into a straight line, and on the pavement on the opposite side of the road she saw an elderly gentleman staring after her, shaking his head at her clumsy and erratic performance. She worked her way up through the gears, heading nowhere in particular, her head pounding with anger and resentment, her swollen and blotchy face awash with a fresh flow of tears. An *old man* standing on the pavement, tut tutting at her driving and shaking his silly superior head from side to side. An *old man*. Bobby would never be an old man. Bobby would never be a granddad with a wife and a dog, a happy retirement with a membership at the golf club. Jesus Christ, she could so easily resent *anyone* purely for being alive whilst Bobby lay dead. It wasn't fair. Where was her beautiful son? Where was her golden boy, her angel, her innocent blonde bundle of sunshine and happiness? What had Bobby done to deserve this - a life so short that it was barely worth having.

Maria slowed down and gave her face a rough wipe with the back of her arm. No, that wasn't true. She mustn't think like that. Bobby's life had been worth every minute, every second. But God, if he'd never been born she wouldn't be going through this torture now. They'd be a happy family of three with Emily in the centre and her and William dancing around their only child like moths around a light bulb. But it hadn't happened like that. They'd begged and pleaded and prayed to any God who would listen for another child. And along came Bobby... dear, sweet Bobby who had made their lives complete. How could it have ended like this? All those years of trying for another baby... then Bobby's arrival... all the gurgling and giggling, the tears, the grazed knees, the first words, the first steps, the first day at school...

six wonderful years of love and laughter, of hopes and dreams for his future, all building up to that one hot August day when he came home from school feeling weak and unwell. What would his future have been if he'd never have caught that dreadful disease? He'd have left school with a good smattering of qualifications… maybe he'd have gone to university, tried cigarettes, got drunk on cheap cider, found a girlfriend, found a decent job, got married, had children of his own… Strange to think there were people out there now whose lives were destined to take a totally different path now that Bobby was dead. Somewhere running around was a little girl who would have been his first girlfriend. Somewhere out there was a little girl who may have become his wife and the mother of his children. They would never know what might have been and all Maria could do was guess.

Suddenly she pulled the car into the car park of The Boatman, a canal side pub boasting outside tables near the tow path. It was either stop there or put her foot down and ram the car so hard into a brick wall there'd be little chance of her surviving. Turning off the engine she gave a large sigh and slumped back in the seat. She felt limp and lifeless, defeated, helpless and totally devoid of energy or inclination to do anything whatsoever. Her breathing was more measured now, more controlled and she felt a sudden wave of guilt at shouting at Emily and William and storming out of the house. How tempting it had been to push the accelerator to the floor and to hell with the consequences. How deep now was the desire to go to sleep and never wake up. What a blessed release it would be. Christ, she couldn't even afford the luxury of killing herself. What about William and Emily? They didn't deserve such a selfish act being forced upon them. The living hell must continue… for their sakes alone she had to continue.

Maria wasn't sure how long she sat there in The Boatman car park but eventually the inside of the car became so suffocatingly hot she had to open the door and step out. Reaching back in she rummaged through the glove box and found an old pair of sunglasses. Then, in the little comfort zone one instantly enters into from the wearing of shades, she went to the bar to order a bitter shandy to drink outside. A hot and sunny Saturday lunchtime in August ensured that all of the outside

Wendy Turner Webster

tables were taken. Maria took a large sip of her shandy and started to stroll along the tow path. There was a wooden bench a little further up just by the lock and she sat on that to finish her drink. Soon a barge glided around the bend in the canal and approached the lock. The barge was a really pretty one with red and green paintwork and fancy gold lettering on the side. 'The Charlotte' it read with 'for holiday hire' details and a registration number underneath. Who was Charlotte? Who had named their barge The Charlotte and then lovingly painted her name on the side? And who was sailing in her now? The need for The Charlotte to negotiate the lock provided Maria with the answer. A man wearing blue denim shorts and a white vest sprang from the barge and set about the business of opening the lock. Two little ginger haired boys, about eight or nine Maria guessed and obviously twins, scrambled up onto the deck and started to shout instructions.

"Faster, dad, faster!"

"Nice work dad, were getting lower already!" And indeed The Charlotte was rapidly sinking to meet the lower water level of the next section of canal.

"Help, were sinking! We're all going to drown!" One of the freckled faced pair screamed out, whilst the other burst into a fit of laughter.

A lady came up onto the deck, wringing out a dishcloth and asking what all the fuss was about. She had long sandy hair tied back in a pony tail and she gave a carefree little giggle as she flicked the wet dishcloth towards her boys.

She looked over towards Maria. "Kids eh? Who'd 'ave 'em?!"

Maria smiled and gave a half wave, safe behind her sunglasses. Shouts and screams and shrieks of laughter faded off into the heat haze of the afternoon and soon The Charlotte was through the lock and on her journey once more, gliding around the canal network with a smiling, happy family on board. But what was waiting for them around the corner, wondered Maria. What disaster might befall any of them tomorrow, next week or next year? What terrible illness or accident might they have to experience, to survive as she had to? One of the twins maybe, leaving his soul mate lost and alone. Oh, they looked happy enough now of course, enjoying lazy summer days on the canal with the sun beating down on their backs. But hadn't Maria's family looked like that once; that glorious week at Woolacombe... Bobby throwing his crusts to the seagulls... Bobby collecting shells and stones in a purple bucket....

Maria wiped a tear away from under her sunglasses as in the distance The Charlotte finally disappeared from view. She drained her glass of the now warm shandy and headed off back towards the car. It was time to go home.

Chapter 10

DARREN O'DOWEL HAD BEEN ON SEVERAL trips courtesy of a tab of acid, but never one like this. This was a really bad trip – the kind of soul destroying, mind altering journey that put you off taking acid for the rest of your life. The image of his father in the cage was still floating before him, misty and distorted one minute, pulling sharply into focus the next. The clown was still there too, leaning on the cage with tears forming a constant drip from his cheeks to the ground. The dialogue between Darren and his father was fragmented, muddled, confused and surreal, yet the words cut through to Darren's heart.

"Look what you've done to me, Darren… you and your slut mother…"

"Must be some keys to the cage, father… Shall I find the keys?"

"I'll kill you if you let me out… you… so disappointing…"

"I've always tried to please you… father… dad…"

"You had an affair with my wife…"

"No! Jeremy… it was Jeremy…"

"Too thick to get into Oxford… that's you… such a crushing disappointment."

And so it went on, until one blessed moment when Darren clearly heard the cry of seagulls overhead and felt Barry's body right up beside him.

"Fucking Christ, man!" Barry was clawing at Darren's chest as his muscles went into painful, involuntary spasms.

Darren starred up at the seagulls and the passing clouds, so relieved to be back on Blackpool beach that he didn't mind Barry's closeness or the discomfort of his own jerking limbs. It was mid evening by the time they could speak to each other and make any degree of sense and even then it was just short bursts of 'never again, man', 'bad trip' and 'never doing that shit again.' Eventually they felt sane enough to make it back to Mrs Holby's Bed & Breakfast. John was already there lying on his bed, unsure of his own movements since the monstrous shoelaces episode a short lifetime ago and in full agreement about it being a 'bad trip' and 'never again'. The oblivion that sleep brought was a merciful release and the following day it was three rather downcast and pale-faced young men who made their way back home to Manchester. Darren didn't see a great deal of his parents but even so, in light of his LSD experience, he was already anticipating with dread how uncomfortable he'd feel when they next met or spoke... memories of his father accusing him of sleeping with his mother... too thick to get into Oxford... looks of pain and hatred – such hatred that Darren didn't mind if he neither saw nor spoke to his parents for a long, long time.

He was hardly relishing the return to his Manchester semi either. After all, it was hardly what you'd call a sanctuary. It was hardly a haven of peace and tranquillity... not when he shared it with Davina – his wife.

✿

Darren O'Dowel and Davina Bailey had met in their first year at Kenhurst University; he was studying physics and engineering, she was struggling with geography and considering dropping out altogether. A whole group of them had decided to go drinking in town one Friday night and Darren and Davina found themselves sitting next to each other on the bus. As a person Darren was no more popular at university than he had been throughout his school years – too brooding, too argumentative, too arrogant to win over many friends. He seemed to have a knack however of always having a small amount of cannabis about his person, with the occasional surprise appearance of the much superior variety – Lebanese black. Where and how he got hold of this continuous supply he kept a closely guarded secret. The basic fact was that he had access to something the rest of them wanted and it was this, rather than any personal attributes, which made him a character worthy of being included. Nevertheless, he found himself sitting alone on the bus until Davina strolled down the aisle towards him.

"Anyone sitting here?" she asked.

"No, take a seat."

"Thanks… God, peace at last! I'm sharing a room with this girl called Susie – she's on the same Geography course as me – and she's moping around like anything because her boyfriend's going off travelling with some of his mates and well, quite frankly, I'm glad to get away from her for a while! My name's Davina by the way, Davina Bailey, first year."

"Darren O'Dowel," he replied, hoping that she wasn't going to prattle on in such a dizzy, brainless manner for the whole fifteen minute journey into town.

Actually, Davina did keep up a constant chitter chatter for the duration of the trip and for the main Darren just let her get on with it, allowing himself to sit back and coolly assess her looks, intelligence and personality. Davina wasn't what you would call a pretty girl, but then again she wasn't bad looking either. She was just rather plain if anything although Darren guessed that she might scrub up well given the right touches of make-up and a decent hair style. As it was her face was scrubbed clean apart from a touch of light pink lip gloss and her dark hair simply hung about her shoulders like a shinny curtain. Darren noted that she had extremely good, clear skin and that her eyes were a dark chocolate brown. Her clothes were the typical baggy hotch potch arrangement generally favoured by first year students but from the smallness of her hands and feet Darren guessed that she was petite and from what he could tell, unfortunately flat chested. Her light banter and almost childish observations certainly didn't suggest to Darren that any great intellect could be attributed to Davina Bailey and he wasn't in the least bit surprised to find out that she was a bit disillusioned with her time at university and was considering maybe swapping courses. Honestly, it was amazing how some people actually got into university in the first place! Still, it was only a geography degree she was studying for – hardly in quite the same league as his physics and engineering course. Darren didn't miss the look of awe and admiration in her eyes when he described some of the finer details of his degree course to her and because it looked good to have a girl on his arm he asked if he could buy her the first drink of the night. She nodded happily at the suggestion and as they got off the bus and headed for the pub which had selected drinks at half price for students he took her hand in his and led her to the bar.

Three beers and two cheap whiskey chasers made Darren look at Davina in a far more favourable light than when he'd first seen her on the bus, and the shedding of several layers of upper body clothing revealed that Davina's womanly features were not as small and uninspiring as Darren had first assumed. She was actually getting more witty and amusing as the night went on and it pleased Darren to see that her chocolate brown eyes were gazing up at his in the same way that a puppy dog might look up at his master.

"Look," he said suddenly, "We don't have to stay in here all night with these losers…"

"No..?" asked Davina, who wasn't quite sure why the group of fellow university students they were with should suddenly be branded as losers.

"I feel we could get to know each other better if we went… somewhere else…"

Davina's senses were suddenly on full sexual alert.

"Did you have anywhere particular in mind?" she asked.

"What about taking the bus back to my place? I've got a small house in Stanford Green…"

"Wow, you've got a house share already? So much cooler than the crappy Halls of Residence I'm stuck in."

Darren savoured the next moment for the impression he knew it would make.

"It's not a house share, actually. I live there by myself. I own the place."

Davina's jaw actually dropped for a second whilst she took in this surprise piece of information. Her gapping mouth and wide-eyed look of total wonderment was exactly what Darren had expected. Thank

Christ for Granny James! Quite why the wrinkly old bat had seen fit to bypass her son Albert and leave her small but adequate estate to her grandson was a question that Darren genuinely didn't know the answer to. He had never been close to the woman. If on the other hand she had done it with the sole intention of severely pissing off Albert then she had certainly succeeded. But as Darren maintained, who was he to question why this stroke of good fortune had come his way? His duty was simply to invest the money in bricks and mortar and to enjoy the benefits of being a first year student with a home he could truly call his own.

"Oh, my God," gushed Davina who had now stopped gapping and found her tongue. "This I've got to see! Let's go!" And they slipped out of the pub whilst the night was still young.

Davina made all the right noises and said all the right things. Darren thought that perhaps she was smarter than he'd first had her down for. For her part Davina rather liked the idea of going out with someone who appeared more of a man than a boy; someone who was quite obviously already on the road to success. The house in Stanford Green was a small but well maintained Victorian terrace – Stanford Green being an area where most of the terraced streets now housed students from the university. Of course the vast majority of the houses had students packed into every available space, but Darren had the luxury of living in splendid isolation. And unlike the others Darren's didn't feature broken and badly stained furniture and the obligatory wine boxes for coffee tables. Some of Granny James' money had gone on a basic range of decent furniture and furnishings – fairly plain and ordinary but well made and matching, and way above the usual student standard.

Darren took Davina into the living room and poured whiskey and ginger ale into two large tumbler glasses. He asked her if she'd like to choose some music from his LP selection whilst he rolled a couple of joints. She sat cross-legged on the floor, spoilt for choice by the range of music on offer whilst Darren sat on the settee and set to work, the clear air of the room quickly giving way to the unmistakable aroma of burning cannabis. Davina eventually settled on David Bowie and then positioned herself beside Darren to take her turn at the joint. The evening had turned out far better than she had expected. To think, she had only joined the group on the bus journey to the pub in order to escape the moaning Susie! The whiskey made her warm and woozy and a deep drag on the joint added to the feeling of contentment. Darren had started talking about English grammar and the appalling misuse of it in modern society. He was so intelligent, so bright, so masterful – surely he'd be bored with her in no time? Still, not if she could help it… not if she could show him a good time and have him begging for more.

Actually it was Darren who made the first move, although making a blatant show of sexual intent was certainly not beyond Davina's capabilities. Play it cool, she thought, play it cool and somewhere between the third joint and the fourth whiskey and ginger she let Darren slip two fingers neatly between her legs. She groaned and wriggled as a third finger suddenly joined the first two and she quickly parted company from her trousers and pants in order to open herself up wider. Christ, thought Darren, this is going to be easier than I thought, and he pushed up her t-shirt so he could examine her tits. Beautiful! OK, not so plump and milky as he would have liked but the nipples themselves were large and pink and fresh and were just begging to be bitten. When Darren did sink his teeth into her flesh Davina screamed in pain, but the hand which wasn't busy between her legs immediately shot up to her mouth and clamped down on it hard. For her part Davina didn't quite know if she was enjoying the experience or not although it was certainly different to the embarrassing fumble on some filthy broken mattress which was usually shared between first year students at Kenhurst.

They had sex right there on the sofa and afterwards smoked John Players, listened to The Doors and finished off the dregs of the whiskey. Darren wouldn't have minded at all if Davina had left then to go back to her own bed, but it soon became apparent that she very much assumed to stay the night with him. Oh well, he thought, what the hell? And they climbed into his double bed and slept like the dead until morning.

Darren was neither happy nor dissatisfied to find Davina by his side a great deal over the following weeks. He was rather indifferent to it in fact although she certainly had her uses. Quite apart from the fact that she seemed agreeable to cooperate in any sexual act he cared to perform on her, she was proving to be a rather good housemaid. She'd do the shopping, sweep the carpet, roll the joints, pour the drinks and scrub the toilet. And she'd even come up with a decent evening meal when the mood took her. Darren did notice that she was hardly attending any of her lectures but then again her subject of geography was somewhat of a joke in comparison to his physics and engineering course. His occasional sneering comments to this effect only served to reinforce Davina's doubts about doing a geography degree at all. Perhaps another course might suit her better? But Darren always had a strong opinion on the subject and said things which seriously made her doubt whether she had the mental capacity to ever be a university graduate. She was beginning to feel a fraud. How had she ever thought she was clever enough to hold her own at a university? Darren had started to hint at the fact that maybe she would be better occupied getting a part time job somewhere local and looking after him. After all, if they were going to stick together it was important that he get a good degree. It was *his* needs that must be considered first. It was *he* that would need total commitment and support. Davina thought about it. Maybe he was right.

By the end of that first year of studies, Davina had officially moved into Darren's terraced house in Stanford Green. Moreover she was no longer a university student but a part time receptionist at the local council planning department. She wouldn't have minded going full time but Darren had been distinctly frosty with her over that suggestion. What was the point of them living together if she wasn't going to around for at least some of the time to look after him? Davina's feelings teetered between a nagging resentment that she always seemed to be bowing to his greater judgement and a pathetic gratefulness that Darren needed her too much to let her go.

It was towards the end of the second year that Darren began to worry that he might not pass his degree course with flying colours after all. Christ, it was difficult. Those lightweight numbskulls doing some crappy history or psychology degree didn't know how easy they'd got it compared to him! His father's reaction to an average result had him breaking out in a cold sweat and shouting at Davina to roll another joint and pour another whiskey. It never occurred to him that the constant drip of cannabis and alcohol that was being fed into his system was actually dulling his natural sharpness, was taking the edge of his intelligence, was making him sluggish when he needed to be razor sharp. Like father like son, Darren's failures and shortcomings could always be blamed on something or someone else; the new lecturer was rubbish, Davina distracted him at crucial study times, his mother would say something to wind him up just when he felt calm and settled. But if Darren had accepted that he wouldn't be the recipient of a double first result, he could never in his worst nightmares have believed that he would come away with a three three grade – an outcome that afterwards made him cringe and squirm whenever he thought about it, or worse still had to admit it to prospective employers.

On his way back from Blackpool to Manchester he let his mind run over that dreadful final year at university and the familiar resentment that boiled up inside him did not bode well for a happy homecoming.

It was a New Year's Eve party that set off the chain of events which Darren would later blame for his disastrous three three result. Against Darren's better judgement Davina had persuaded him to open up their house for a New Year's Eve party. Davina enjoyed showing off the fact that they had a decent home of their own and not some rented hovel, although she rarely got the chance. Darren's dark and brooding looks would easily put off Davina's friends from visiting again. He had a knack for putting people on edge and creating an uneasy atmosphere which most of Davina's girlfriends were glad to escape from. His eyes could look almost black given the right lighting and they'd hold a stare at someone for just a second too long. Anyone could suddenly find themselves on the receiving end of his sarcastic wit, their own good manners or more often sheer embarrassment ensuring a polite little laugh and a quick exit. Still, a party was a party and Davina did a good job in persuading a fairly large group of people to see in the

New Year with them. Not only that but her Aunty Rene and Uncle Mike said they'd pop in early for a quick drink. But even before any of their guests arrived she knew that the whole idea had been a huge mistake. In an effort to be the perfect hostess she had filled several small bowls with crisps and peanuts and dotted them around the living room and kitchen, fanning out some red paper napkins with great attention to detail and placing mats and coasters all over the place to avoid an array of unsightly ring marks. Prior to that she'd spent most of the day scrubbing and cleaning, tidying and polishing until Darren complained that he couldn't even sit down in his own home for fear of making it untidy again. Eventually he poured himself a large whiskey and ginger and rolled himself a joint, taking them and himself out into the back yard to enjoy in peace. Having finished, he went back into the kitchen to pour another drink and sneered long and loud at Davina's efforts with the crisps and peanuts.

"It's pathetic! Who do you think's coming – frigging royalty?"

"Of course not, I just thought it'd be nice to… Oh Darren, you've brought dirt in on your shoes!"

"Well, you know where the floor cloths are kept," he replied and he kicked off his shoes and headed upstairs to the bathroom.

When he came down the kitchen floor had been cleaned once more and Davina was busying herself with glasses and ashtrays.

"Sorry about the skid marks in the toilet," he smirked. "Still, I bet old Aunty Rene's seen some in her time, eh?!"

Davina felt her eyes begin to swim with tears. "Why are you being like this, Darren?" She pleaded, "Why are you being so nasty?"

He shrugged and sauntered off into the living room, taking a large gulp of whiskey on the way. At that point the front door bell rang and Davina composed herself in time to open the door with a flourish and a beaming smile.

"Aunty Rene, Uncle Mike, how lovely to see you. Come on in!"

The sharp noise of breaking glass came from the living room. Davina and her relations entered to find the shattered tumbler and the sticky remains of its contents all over the hearth and about a hundred peanuts scattered on the carpet from one end of the room to the other. Darren held up his bleeding hand and an imaginary glass, his black eyes boring into the three people hovering awkwardly by the door, his lips curling to form the familiar sarcastic smile.

"Happy bloody New Year…"

Unfortunately for Davina the New Year celebrations did not get any better. Predictably, everyone there drank too much and, predictably, the house got totally wrecked. By three o'clock in the morning she neither knew nor cared what was going on downstairs. She'd staggered up to bed some twenty minutes beforehand but, unable to lose consciousness, was now on her knees in front of the toilet, miserably puking up peanuts and crisps and copious amounts of whiskey and cheap fizzy wine. Christ, this was the last time… she'd thrown up on the pavement outside the pub after closing time just three nights ago. Darren had said something really embarrassing about her new hair cut and to blur the pain she'd felt in front of her friends she'd downed three double whiskies in record time. She'd had to forgive him though… he was under such pressure in his final year… and he was so smart and clever – much more so than her. Leaning over the toilet Davina's face was hot and clammy and her hair now stuck to her cheeks and forehead in messy wet clumps. Some of her sick was clinging to the bottom lengths of her hair, a sight which made her cry afresh, and through the tears she could make out Darren's skid marks still streaking down the porcelain. After another half hour of heaving and spitting out the last remnants of bile, she trudged miserably back off to bed.

Davina was surprised and so utterly grateful to be woken on New Year's Day by Darren's fingers working at a furious pace between her legs. He'd made it quite clear to Davina that he didn't want a house full of people and she knew she should have listened to him. He'd got so drunk and loud and aggressive last night that she'd dreaded what mood she was going to wake up to the next day. It was all her fault, but now, *thank God*, he was making love to her, needing her once more. And when he came inside her she almost cried with relief.

It was some ten weeks later that she found herself in the doctor's surgery crying with fright and disbelief.

"It's impossible… just impossible… I've been on the pill for ages! That's safe, isn't it? Practically one hundred percent safe?"

"Well, yes," replied Dr Sanga, passing Davina a tissue. "But think back… have you been on any other medication? Have you been sick at all? Actually vomited on any occasion… let's see the dates… around the New Year maybe?"

Davina stared at Dr Sanga as she remembered and she felt her face burning red with shame. She'd been sick several times around then… and she'd been so sick with all the New Year's Eve drinking that she couldn't even be sure she'd taken the pill at all the following day. So, she'd thrown it up after the party, forgotten to take it the next day and Darren had come inside her. Jesus, that was it – mystery solved. But all the why and how and where and when questions didn't really matter. What mattered was that she was definitely pregnant. What mattered was, *how would Darren react?*

Davina walked home slowly, going over all the different ways she might break the news. God, what if he wanted her to get rid of it, have an abortion? It was unthinkable. After all, this could be the making of them, couldn't it? This would really cement their relationship… a baby may really soften Darren up… calm him down, even. As Davina turned the corner into their road she suddenly had a rosy image of herself being treated like a goddess, a princess; a precious vessel holding priceless jewels. She felt older and wiser now too. Her friends may want to go out every night and get blind drunk, wake up in an unfamiliar bed with a head full of aches and regrets. But her new life would be a world apart from that kind of childish, immature behaviour. They would be a family… a proper family with real commitment.

As soon as Davina entered their house and closed the door behind her she knew this would not be a good time to break the news of her condition to Darren. She could already sense the tension in the atmosphere. Some houses or homes oozed love and warmth or at least a sense of peace and quiet when you entered them. Darren's house, on the other hand, was one of those that could make you feel distinctly uncomfortable the very moment you stepped inside and Davina's stomach lurched as she felt her skin prickle with the anticipation of conflict.

"Oh, fucking hell!" Darren's curse came loud and clear from the living room, confirming Davina's prediction.

Davina tried to creep upstairs but Darren had already heard the front door bang closed.

"Get me a whiskey will you? And you might start some tea while you're at it – I'm frigging starving. Where the hell have you been anyway?"

Davina hesitated before walking into the living room and lying, "Only up to the shops."

"So where are the bags? Where's the shopping?"

"Oh, well… I didn't end up buying anything."

"Bloody hell! I'm working my balls off here while you swan off up to the shops and then can't even be arsed to bring back a pack of cigarettes. I *told* you we were running low. There's no milk in the fucking fridge either. I'll just work every hour God sends *and* trot down to the shops, shall I?"

"I work too…"

"Work?! You call what you do *work*? Christ, someone should have you arrested under the Trade Descriptions Act!" He made a gesture to encompass all of his study books and papers laid out on the table. "*This* is work! Having you as a fucking girlfriend is *work*!"

Davina cried and stumbled into the kitchen, determined to rustle up something quickly to try and appeal to Darren's stomach and put him in a better mood. All this stress he was under… making him say all these cruel things. His finals couldn't come quick enough for Davina. Then they could really start to live properly, really start to prepare for the baby. On a tray Davina placed a glass of whiskey and ginger with ice alongside a plate heaped with toast, spaghetti in tomato sauce and two fried eggs. She picked it up, held her head high and walked in to the living room where Darren was still pouring over his studies.

She kicked open the door with her foot.

"Darren, some food…"

"Not now," he muttered, "I'm just working out the last bit of this formula."

"Well, I'll just leave it here…"

Davina made to cross the room to put the tray down on the coffee table but before she had barely taken a step one of Darren's largest and heaviest physics text books had struck her on the side of the head. He roared and leapt up out of his chair as the hardback found its mark.

"You stupid bitch! I was trying to concentrate!"

The tray and all that it carried fell to the floor. Darren's training shoes mashed the spaghetti and eggs into the carpet as he reached out for Davina's hair and yanked her head backwards, all the time screaming out like a wounded animal. Davina fell back against the wall and he was still gripping her hair as they slid together to the floor. Darren's eyes were glazed and his screams turned to sobs of rage and self pity.

"All this work… I'm under so much pressure… so much fucking pressure…"

Davina eyes were closed as she whimpered over and over again, "Please don't hurt me Darren. I love you. Please don't hurt me or the baby…"

On and on she feverishly whispered the words until she felt Darren's grip on her hair suddenly loosen. He gripped her face with both hands and his wild eyes bored into hers.

"Oh God, I'm so sorry… what have I done? Please forgive me. I'm so sorry. I'm so sorry. I love you. Don't leave me. Don't take the baby away. I'm begging you, Davina, not to take my baby away. I'm so sorry."

They lay there for some time, amongst the toast and the eggs and the ice cubes, allowing the tomato sauce of the spaghetti to stain their clothes, oblivious to the whiskey and ginger that was soaking though to their skin. Because of Darren's assurances Davina grew increasingly confident that she had just witnessed a side of him that she would never see again. And when he drew himself up onto one knee and asked her to marry him, she thought that all her troubles were over.

Darren O'Dowel and Davina Bailey were married at the local registry office just six weeks later. Darren chose a fellow university student called Michael Sheldon to be his best man whilst Davina opted for her rather sulky fourteen year old sister as her only bridesmaid. Both sets of parents attended the ceremony and managed, for the sake of the occasion, to be civil to each other throughout. Neither condoned this liaison. Neither was happy about the permanent match that was now being made. Albert secretly marvelled at the fact that his son could have got himself trapped by this little airhead in such an obviously calculated way, whilst Mrs Bailey smiled a false smile and wondered what on earth her pretty daughter saw in this hard-nosed, arrogant, peevish youth she was now kissing before the registrar. And what in God's name was she thinking of, getting herself pregnant by him? Mrs Bailey's false smile faded and she visibly slumped as she envisaged herself years into the future, still picking up the pieces from this quite dreadful coupling.

Elsa took out her handkerchief and dabbed at the corner of her eyes in an attempt to show some emotion – that was what mothers did at weddings, wasn't it? She wasn't sure. Was she going over the top? She sneaked a glance at Mrs Bailey. She wasn't crying, she was smiling! What on earth was there to smile about, a pretty girl like that getting completely bogged down at such a young age? And she knew her son... she knew only too well his cruelty, his arrogance, his bitterness. Did others who came into contact with him sense what she knew? Mrs Bailey should be weeping with pity if she'd got any sense. Christ, she needed a drink. How soon could they get out of this suffocating place so she could order the gin and tonic that would make her feel instantly better?

Mr Bailey too was ready for a drink – a large brandy would slip down rather well right now. And then another one and then perhaps another one after that. Still, better keep it under control or that cocky sonofabitch that was now his son-in-law could find himself with a black eye and a bloody nose. God, it was difficult smiling your way through all this when inside you were consumed with disappointment and fury. That bugger had got his little girl pregnant! Pregnant - the very thought of it! Him touching her, undressing her, getting an erection and.... He let out an audible groan. He couldn't bear the thought of the two of them together but here they were in front of him, being pronounced man and wife. Now he really, *really* needed a brandy.

As tradition dictated, Mr Bailey settled the fees for the registry office and paid the bar and restaurant bill for their post wedding celebration. But much to his annoyance Darren flatly (and quite rudely) refused his offer to pay for a honeymoon, giving him an almost pompous speech about how only 100% application and dedication to his studies was on the agenda for the following few weeks, leading up to his finals at Kenhurst University. He could never have foreseen that his studies and subsequent exams would be a spectacular fiasco due to Davina's miscarriage. Recently married and just five months pregnant, Davina come round from a heavy sleep one morning with a feeling of warmth and stickiness between her legs. For a few minutes she wallowed in the grogginess of her half awake, half asleep state, until she forced her eyes open and confronted the alarm bells ringing in her head. She threw back the duvet, fully aware of what she was about to see. Blood. There was blood everywhere; deep maroon, almost black where it had dried into the cotton sheets and bright, glistening red where it had most recently seeped and then gushed out from inside her. She tried to get up but her legs were too weak to carry her.

"Darren! Darren!"

Darren came into the room and stared at the bloody scene.

"Fucking hell!" he shouted and ran back downstairs.

Davina wept and prayed for her unborn baby as Darren telephoned for an ambulance, but in her heart she already knew it was a lost cause. She finally lost the baby in the ambulance as it sped towards the hospital, blue lights flashing and sirens blaring. She stayed in the hospital for two nights, thinking about her baby, thinking about Darren, thinking what might have been. When she arrived home, wobbly and tearful she was greeted by the sight of the blood stained bedding bundled up in a heap on the kitchen floor.

"You insensitive bastard!" she screamed. "You might have washed them, you know… you might have burned them or thrown them away or torn yourself away from your books for five minutes to have done *something* with them!"

Darren slammed down the whiskey bottle on the kitchen work surface.

"Well that's fucking rich! Thanks to marrying you and all this latest fiasco I can't concentrate on anything to do with this fucking degree. Christ, we needn't even have bothered getting married!"

Darren poured himself a good half tumbler full of whiskey and topped it up with ginger ale before stamping out of the kitchen and slamming the door behind him. Davina stood rooted to the spot, crying bitter lonely tears – unable to stop and unable to make sense of the dire situation she'd found herself in with Darren O'Dowel. It was some time later that she finally blew her nose and picked up the bloody sheets from the floor. She pushed them all inside the drum of the washer and closed the door, wondering for the first time whether marrying Darren had been a huge and utter mistake.

Chapter 11

Darren turned his key in the front door of his and Davina's semi-detached house on the southern outskirts of Manchester and knew straight away there was going to be trouble. It was early afternoon on a Thursday and The Rolling Stones were thundering out of the speakers in the front room. The smell of cannabis hit him as soon as he stepped into the hall and he heard the laughter of Davina and her best friend, Rachel – cackling together like two witches brewing up spells.

He went into the lounge and looked at Davina.

"What the hell are you doing home?"

"Well, that's a nice way to greet you wife, I must say!" giggled Rachel.

"Fuck off out of my house, Rachel." Darren's black eyes met hers and she immediately started scuttling around for her belongings, muttering something about it being time she was making a move anyway.

Davina's eyes were glazed over from the effects of whiskey and cannabis but she hadn't missed the subtlety of Darren's last words.

"*My* house, *my* house?" she shouted. "It's *our* house!"

"Not for much fucking longer."

Rachel said a hasty 'goodbye' and fled the scene.

"What's that meant to mean? And never mind *what am I doing home* – I pulled a sickie if you must know. Couldn't stand that old bitch of an office manager on my back again all day. And anyway, how can a stag party last for five frigging days?!"

"Well it did…"

"Your dad called a couple of days ago by the way…"

Darren winced at the thought and mention of his father.

"I told him to try calling the radio station – see if they knew where you were. We had quite a chat… of course, he still can't understand why you're bumming around as a radio engineer when you're obviously so clever you could do a lot better for yourself. I had to remind him there's only so much a person can do if they haven't got any qualifications…"

Davina's speech was slurred and her manner was sneering and of course she had no idea of the recent interaction Darren had had with his father courtesy of a tab of acid.

"Take your things and get out of my house, *now*."

"I told you, it's *our* house."

Darren screamed and lurched towards her, grabbing her by the scruff of the neck and manhandling her towards the front door.

"I can't stand you any longer," he screamed in her face. "I can't bare the sight of you, you fucking little bitch, get out!"

He tried to shove her out of the house but Davina fought back, clawing and grasping at the door frame. Darren drew back his fist and with an accurate aim to the face punched her away from him, away from the house and out of his life. Davina had been like a mill stone around his neck for the last four years… like a leech, sapping his life blood, bleeding him dry. She held him back, sneered at his work, questioned his authority. She was a fucking little sponge and he deserved better. Yes, he deserved a much, much better wife than this.

Davina Bailey lay dazed on the front path with a bleeding eye and a broken cheek bone. Slowly, she raised her head and looked into Darren's eyes. Two black currants stared back at her; two black currants imbedded in an ugly doughy white face. Her heart contracted with pain and fear, and love for her husband.

Chapter 12

FOLLOWING THE DEATH OF A LOVED one, the grieving relatives must endure a series of painful 'firsts'… a first Valentine's, a first birthday, a first Easter, a first holiday… but in the case of the death of a child it is surely the first Christmas without them which is the hardest, most awful time to bare. Maria, William and Emily had that to come but their first 'first' was only just around the corner – the beginning of a new school term – the first day back at school without Bobby, and towards the end of the summer holidays they began to brace themselves for the day when the new school year would begin. Emily had asked if she could go to the shops with Karen to get some new school clothes and Maria was more than happy to hand over some money and let the girls loose on a school uniform shopping adventure. Maria breathed a sigh of relief as she watched the girls trot off into Dawson's - the town's one and only department store. They'd been given strict instructions to meet up with her again in one hour, so with time on her hands she headed for the self service cafeteria. Thank God for young girls revelling in the excitement of being allowed to buy their own school clothes. Thank God she'd been spared the ordeal of walking into the school uniform section of the children's department, past the rows of little grey shorts and snowy white vests, past the 'value packs' of boys' underpants and knee high socks, past all the things she would have being buying for Bobby, had he still been alive.

The End of Emily West

The coolness of the department store offered considerable relief from the steaming heat outside – the hottest summer anyone could remember wasn't ready to give way yet. En route to the cafeteria Maria cast a disinterested eye over a rail of cheesecloth tops. How silly and trivial everything seemed nowadays; embroidered cheesecloth tops, a mannequin dressed head to toe in a blaze of tartan offering shoppers the chance to show allegiance to The Bay City Rollers, Abba on the tannoy system singing in perfect harmony about a 'dancing queen'. Maria was still gazing at the vision in tartan when Dancing Queen merged smoothly into 'Don't Go Breaking My Heart'. She sighed and continued on her path… what on earth did Elton John and Kiki Dee know about broken hearts? Had either of them lost a little blonde angel called Bobby? Did they really know what it was like to have your heart ripped out of your body and smashed to smithereens? What were they singing about anyway – some stupid failed relationship? Well they could take their number one single and ram it down their bloody throats! Maria picked up a tray from the pile and banged it down on the wide metal ledge in front of her.

"Yes, love," said the lady serving behind the counter. "What can I get you? Scones are back on today…"

Maria looked up at her, momentarily startled by her question.

"Oh, er…no, nothing to eat thank you… just coffee, a pot of coffee please…" she replied, her anger towards Elton John and Kiki Dee slowly subsiding as she set about the business of unzipping her purse and finding some money to pay for the coffee.

Once seated safely in a quiet corner Maria sipped her coffee and leafed through a newspaper which a previous customer had left behind. She read the words describing chronic water shortages and studied the pictures of emergency standpipes in Yorkshire but absorbed neither. Eventually, non the wiser as to the day's news, she folded up the paper and plonked it back down on the table. What a bloody coward she was, not even able to pull herself together to buy Emily a few new school clothes. What an underhand, cowardly act it had been to shove some pound notes at her and let her get on with it, to abandon her to her own devices at a time when a mother's judgement was so obviously needed. It might suit Karen Black's mum but it didn't suit her and she squirmed in her seat as she imagined Emily and Karen picking out the wrong items in the wrong sizes, or worse still going off at a complete tangent and spending their money on everything tartan!

After spinning out the consumption of one pot of coffee for fifty minues, Maria gathered up her coat and bag and purposefully headed towards the school uniform department. It had been ridiculous to try and let them buy their new school clothes on their own and doubtless she'd find them there clutching a wide assortment of unsuitable garments. It was time to be brave. It was time to march straight in there, help the girls make their choices and come straight back out again. There was simply no need to linger around the stuff intended for little school boys. But when she got to the uniform section there was no sign of Emily or Karen. A shop assistant saw her stop and hesitate and came up to her.

"Can I help you at all, Madam," she asked.

"Yes…er… I'm looking for my daughter… she's meant to be coming here with her friend to choose some new school clothes. Perhaps they're looking in some other departments first…"

"Well, there were two young ladies here who bought some school clothes," said the shop assistant. "One of them was wearing a bright red jacket, a red hat…"

"Yes!" pounced Maria, "That's my daughter!"

"…And very good choices the two of them made if I may say so… quite grown up they both were. I helped them with the sizes of course. So polite they were too… left only about five minutes ago I should say."

Maria suddenly felt rather deflated. She hadn't really been needed after all.

The shop assistant rambled on. "So sensible they were with the money they'd got… I showed them the special offer on the navy blue skirts with the box pleat and they took one of those each… we've got that offer on the boys' shorts and long trousers too… those are all over in *that* isle…"

Maria thanked her and walked away, trying in vain to focus her mind on the cosmetics counters she could see in the distance. *Boys' shorts and long trousers, boys' shorts and long trousers.* A barrage of different perfumes assaulted her senses as she hit the sanctuary of the Estee Lauder counter and on complete autopilot she chose and paid for two lipsticks and a revolutionary new night cream. She pocketed the change and had a sudden and terrifying vision of taking Emily to school on the first day of term; other parents avoiding her eye, other parents unable to witness her grief, other parents with exactly the same number of children they had had at the end of the last term. *Boys' shorts and long trousers, boys' shorts and long trousers.* How was she meant to take one child to school, when she was meant to be taking two?

Being the kind and considerate husband and father that he was, William foresaw the pain and terror that the first day back at school would bring and so booked himself a day off work in order to escort Maria and Emily to the school gates. He rallied round and managed some carefree banter with Emily over the breakfast table, finally bringing out his camera to record the momentous occasion of her first day as a 'senior'. Maria gritted her teeth and tried to conceal her blotched skin with foundation cream and powder. So much for that revolutionary new moisturiser. She brushed her hair, tugging at it savagely before tying it back in a tight ponytail. She felt old and ugly, worn out and washed out and couldn't wait until the school run was over so she could crawl back into bed. Not for her the coffee and pastry at the local cafe when the school bell had gone, catching up with the other mums, sharing stories of the summer holidays, laughing that they'd been far too long, laughing that they were glad to get the little terrors back to school at last. Not for her the gossip at the school gates, the speculation as to who would be the new class rep' or the new chair person of the PTA. None of that mattered now, none of it felt the least bit relevant to her anymore and once again she thought of the bed that was waiting for her to return to, and of the glorious moment when she could pull the sheets over her face and find sanctuary in the darkness. And when the day was over she could tick this 'first' off the list, for it would never come again. What a blessed relief that it would never come again. All she had to do from tomorrow was endure the next run of 'firsts' that the following months would bring… the first half term holiday without Bobby, the first halloween, the first bonfire night and then the nightmare one, the killer – the one which would surely send her to her grave if she didn't pull herself round for the sake of William and Emily – the first Christmas.

Chapter 13

IT WOULD BE MISLEADING TO SAY that Emily felt any degree of the kind of pain that Maria and William felt in those last few months of 1976, because quite simply, she did not. It wasn't that she didn't care, or that Rascal or The Rubettes or The Bay City Rollers were more important, or that she was so hard-hearted she didn't feel the pain of Bobby's death; it was because she had been so successful in building up her defences. She had quickly learnt that if she didn't let herself think about Bobby then she could not feel sad about him. If she forced herself to dismiss his memory then she could get on with her life without ever having to face up to or acknowledge her loss. It was easier that way. It was easier to live and easier to survive. Of course at the age of eleven it never occurred to her that one day in the future she would let the memory of Bobby break free and it would all come crashing down around her. One doesn't know these things at eleven. One doesn't realise the consequences of locking things away.

By the time the bonfire night celebrations came about Emily had easily settled into her new life in the first year of the senior school and she and Karen Black were closer than ever, taking on the enormity of the 'big' school with as much bravado as two bright eleven year olds could muster. Paul Andrew had, quite naturally, got his own circle of male pals to kick around with, but outside school he made the occasional visit to Whitemoor Farm and in general made Emily feel rather good about herself.

On the Thursday evening before the local bonfire and firework display on the Saturday, William came home from work armed with several packets of sparklers. Emily was locked away in her bedroom studying for a history test the next day.

"Hello, love," he said, walking up to Maria in the kitchen and giving her a kiss on the cheek. "Picked up these from the newsagents. We can take them with us on Saturday night."

Maria gave a "Mmm," of indifference as she flicked on the switch to boil the kettle.

"There were about a dozen people piling up stuff on that bonfire when I just drove past... old chairs, old tables, even an old five barred gate - you wait 'til you see it! Must be double the size of last year..."

"If you say so..."

"Come on love," William coaxed, "It'll be fun... I know Emily's really looking forward to it..."

"Well I'm not," Maria replied sulkily. "I don't look forward to anything anymore. Why don't the two of you go on your own and I'll have the night in."

William's cheerful mask suddenly fell away and he looked at her coldly, the home truths which had been dancing on the tip of his tongue for so long now ready to be told.

"Have you any idea, at all, how utterly selfish you sound? How utterly selfish and unfair you're being to me and Emily?"

Maria swung round to face him ready to do battle, ready to scream obscenities about the unfairness of it all. But the words stuck in her throat as surely as the tears welled up and poured down her face and she sank onto the kitchen floor in a crumpled, defeated heap.

"I know I'm horrible," she sobbed, "I know I'm being a selfish, horrible cow to you and Emily... I know you miss Bobby as much as I do... Oh God, Bobby... oh God..."

Maria's voice was distorted through the sobs and she began to rock back and forth as William got down on the floor beside her and took her head in his hands.

"Look at me, Maria," he said. "*Look at me.*" And he forced her head up to be in line with his, for his eyes to be in direct contact with hers.

"We've got to carry on…" William's voice was low, urgent and desperate in an effort to make his words hit their mark. "We've got no choice… we've got no bloody choice but to carry on. Don't you see? Don't you think I've wanted to end it all… put an end to all this pain and misery?"

William's voice cracked. "I've been dying inside, Maria… dying inside because Bobby's gone, but I have to keep going for you and for Emily… and you have to keep going for us… you have to be strong and keep going because we can't survive without you…"

William's face was flushed with emotion as they held on to each other, drawing strength from the vice like grip of this desperate embrace. Eventually William got to his feet and pulled Maria to hers and they spent a long time just holding on to each other, finding what little comfort they could.

Eventually Maria sighed and said, "Of course we'll all go to the bonfire on Saturday… of course we will…"

"I know it won't be easy," said William, "Christ, nothing is at the moment, is it? But we'll take these ruddy sparklers and go to the ruddy bonfire and for Emily's sake we'll have a bloody cheerful look on our faces!"

And for the first time in a long time Maria managed the briefest of smiles.

So, the long ago boiled kettle was switched on once more and some semblance of normality prevailed in the West household. Emily broke off from her history revision to come downstairs for a cup of coffee before Maria set about the business of making them all something to eat, and William showed Emily the packs of sparklers and told her too about the now colossal proportions of the local bonfire. True to form Emily didn't allow herself to think of how much Bobby would have enjoyed examining the sparklers, how excited he would have been about the notion of a bonfire so gigantic it had to be seen to be believed. Those thoughts were secret, were to be locked away for another time… they weren't to be aired here in the kitchen, causing upset when a bright and cheery façade would serve the moment so much better. More feelings crushed down and suppressed until such a time that the bomb of Bobby's memory would explode into a thousand pieces.

There must have been over five hundred people standing around the fire on that Saturday night. Emily, Maria and William had chosen a spot at the front – the closest to the fire one could stand without the heat of the flames actually burning one's cheeks. The smell of the burning wood with its earthy, mossy undertones mingled with the fatty fumes from the chip van and hot dog stand – an unmistakable combination of aromas immediately identifiable as bonfire night. Emily looked over her shoulder and surveyed the crowd; a mass of faces – glowing orange disks basking in the heat of the fire, gazing upwards as if worshipping the sun itself. Turning back she looked at the Guy strapped into an old armchair, balanced precariously on top of the old tables, tree branches, bits of old fencing and any other piece of flammable material that made up the magnificent bonfire. Whoever had made the Guy Fawkes figure had taken some pride in the job. It was life-sized and wore a suitable array of jumble sale clothes; work trousers, thick-soled boots, a shirt and a battered old suit jacket. Its enormous papier mache head wore a black wig topped with a trilby hat and its carefully painted eyes stared back at the crowd as the relentless flames started to lick at the legs of the chair. William went off in search of some chips and Maria put her arm around Emily as the Guy's boots succumbed to the heat and began to burn.

"I feel sorry for him, mum… it's horrible," said Emily, although even as she spoke the words she found it difficult to look away. There was something rather hypnotic about watching the flames slowly devour the straw filled body.
"I know," agreed Maria, "It is rather gruesome… what a way to go. Thank goodness we don't dispose of people like that nowadays!"
By the time William returned with the chips and ketchup the Guy Fawkes doll was engulfed in flames. Cheers went up as it and the armchair slumped forward in a sudden crackle of sparks and splintered wood. Emily had a vision of another fire on another night all those

years ago – a fire that burned the real Guy Fawkes, surrounded by people baying for his blood. And with a slight shiver in spite of the ferocious heat of the flames she imagined how that Guy Fawkes would have screamed out in agony as the fire burnt into his flesh.

When the chips were all finished William produced the sparklers. Karen Black and her parents and a couple more friends from school found their way over to Emily and the grown-ups looked on indulgently as the girls used the fizzing, spitting sticks to write their names in the dark. The last of the sparklers had barely gone out when the first firework of the night went off – a rocket which whistled up into the air at breakneck speed before exploding into a starburst of electric blues and greens. This is what the crowd had come for, this riot of colour and noise and there didn't seem to be a rocket, banger, screamer or starburst which didn't get their cheer of approval - each new offering from the skies above appearing to be more deserving of their whoops of joy than the last.

When they arrived home William put on some toast for their supper. Then he and Emily carefully analysed the firework display and re-lived some of their best moments whilst Maria fussed around with plates and jam and napkins and occasionally chipped into the conversation. Emily had been forced to grow up since the beginning of August. If Bobby was still alive now the scene would be totally different… instead of sitting upright on the settee commenting on the evening she would probably be running all over the place with her younger brother, shouting, teasing, hugging, fighting, pretending to be fireworks – being a child. She wouldn't be sitting here like this, chit chatting politely, on best behaviour so as not to give her mum and dad anything more to worry over or be sad about. Eventually, with a feeling of anticlimax instead of elation, Emily said goodnight and went off to bed, the machine gun fire sounds of the bangers still ringing in her ears. William stayed up with the television for company and gave in to the temptation of more toast and jam. Maria took off her make-up, put on her nightie and slumped into bed, thankful once again that another wretched 'first' was over. And tonight, as with most nights, she buried her face into the pillow and cried herself to sleep.

Chapter 14

THE FIRST SNOW OF THAT WINTER fell whilst Emily was at Whitemoor Farm one Sunday afternoon in early December, mucking out Rascal's stable. Rascal was standing at the top of the field in his thick winter New Zealand rug, edging his way closer to the gate in anticipation of his tea time meal of chopped carrots, pony nuts and warm bran mash. Emily stopped her muck shovelling for a minute or two to watch this sudden change in the weather, grateful of the excuse to rest her weary limbs and lean out over the stable door. The sky above was thick and grey and heavy with snow. The snow that afternoon fell steadily – large flakes which were destined to stick and form a white blanket rather then the small, half-hearted variety that quickly and disappointingly soon turned to rain and then slush. No, this was the real thing – picture postcard snow, a Christmas card land where snowmen with top hats and carrot noses live and would-be ice-skaters don their boots and take to the local pond. In this winter wonderland of glittering frost and endless magic Santa Clause delivers mountains of presents to little boys and girls who live in the prettiest of country cottages... carol singers with brightly knitted scarves and bobble hats sing around the cheerful glow of old fashioned oil lamps and Victorian children push their little pink noses up against the windows of Victorian sweet shops. Emily smiled and got back to work, thinking how a fall of snow before Christmas can make the heart beat faster in anticipation of some longed for festive magic, just like they *surely* used to enjoy in the old days.

By the time Emily had finished laying down fresh straw in Rascal's stable, piling it up thick in the middle and banking it up high at the sides, it was already white over outside. The greys and browns of the stable yard had disappeared to be replaced by a dazzling white layer of proper winter snow. And the snow clouds were as thick and as heavy as ever – the giant flakes kept falling and the snow on the ground just got thicker and thicker. Emily led Rascal into his stable and scolded him for immediately peeing on his new straw bed.

"Honestly," she said to him as she changed his wet outdoor rug for a padded indoor one, "I really don't know why I bother!"

Rascal ignored her sharp tone and simply pawed at the ground, snorting and demanding food.

"Ok, ok," she grinned, "It's coming!" And soon his warm, peachy soft nose was snuffling around in a large bowl of warm mash.

"He's as 'appy as a pig in muck!" said Mr Johnson as he leant over the stable door. "Aye, just look at this stable. If Mrs Johnson ever gets fed up of me I'd be quite grateful to spend the night 'ere on this bed!"

"Oh, I don't think so, Mr Johnson! The first thing Rascal did was pee in it…"

"Don't worry love" said Mr Johnson, laughing at the indignant look on Emily's face, "They all do that… it's just their way of saying they appreciate the lovely bed what you've just spent two hours making for 'em! Anyway, I've come over to tell you that your daddy's just rung… worried he is about all this snow so I've told him not to be 'cos I'll run you back up home in the Land Rover. Mrs Johnson's just making some hot chocolate for you so I'll see you in the kitchen in a few minutes, alright?"

Emily smiled and nodded and felt her stomach rumble at the thought of the hot chocolate. Five minutes later she was crossing the yard to the house, enjoying making fresh footprints in the virgin snow. Who can resist the childish urge to look back at the path one's made on a blank canvas of snow? When Emily got to the door to the house she looked back, and for one brief and unsettling moment she remembered looking at another set of footprints… ones that were much smaller than hers… a set of perfect little footprints in the clear golden sands of Woolacombe beach.

At Oakside Grange William had settled down in one of the arm chairs to watch a Western film on the TV. In the kitchen Maria sat eating chocolate cake with her friend, Fiona, who was now looking out of the window at the snow, grateful for the fact she drove a Range Rover, albeit six years old with eighty thousand miles on the clock.

"Bloody hell, Maria, that old Rover might just come into its own today! Oh yes, go on then – just one more piece. Mine's playing darts and yours is watching a Western so what else are we meant to do but scoff chocy cake? Are you alright love? You've gone a bit pale…"

"Sorry Fiona… I was just thinking… would you, well the fact is… would you come up to Bobby's room with me? Please..?"

"God, yes, of course… *of course* I will. Is it… well, is it all…"

"Yes, it's still as it was. I haven't touched it and there's never going to be a good time to do it. But I don't want it to become some kind of shrine and I don't want his room to become some musty, untouchable place which has to be left intact in case he might return. Oh shit, I don't know what to do for the best."

Fiona moved over to Maria and held both her hands in hers.

"OK, this is what we'll do… let's go up there now for just a few minutes and you can see what you feel like doing with the room. We can make some plans and then tomorrow, if you're feeling up to it we can sort through it together and maybe box some stuff up and put it in the loft."

"Of course," said Maria, "We can store it in the loft. I just can't image trying to part with any of his stuff…"

"And no one's asking you to," said Fiona, gently. "Come on…"

Maria heard the thunderous sound of hooves and gunfire coming from the lounge and felt a twinge of guilt that she was entering the sanctity of Bobby's room with her friend and not her husband. But what was the point of putting William through it? Fiona was detached –

The End of Emily West

sympathetic obviously – but even so detached from the acute heartache of the situation. Fiona would be strong, tactful, forthright and tell her what in the world she should do with the toys, books, clothes and photos that made up the few short years of Bobby's life.

His room was warm and stuffy – that was the first thing that struck Maria as she opened the door and stepped inside. The surfaces were dusty on account of not having been cleaned for months and the place had a stale air about it – the stale air of a room that had not been lived in for some time. The room felt sad and empty, the atmosphere as dead as the little boy who had once slept there. Fiona surveyed the scene, trying to concentrate on how many boxes they would need. Maria sat down heavily on the bed and reached over to the pile of books on the bedside table. Mary, Mongo and Midge, The Adventures of Tom and Jerry, Hector's House pop-up book…

"There are tonnes more books under this bed," said Maria suddenly. "We'll need a big box for all the books."

"Yes," replied Fiona, and then trying to be practical, "And I should think we'll need two or three large ones for toys… two for clothes…"

William put his head around the door with a barely audible, "Everything alright, love?"

Maria nodded, noting that William has asked the question with all the timid reserve of someone used to violent reactions and hysterical outbursts.

"Oh, William," said Fiona, her voice sounding falsely bright and loudly out of place in the silent dusty bedroom, "I was going to give Maria a hand with sorting out some of Bobby's things…"

"That's kind of you, Fiona," he said, more confident now that this delicate situation was under control, "Thanks for helping out… very kind."

"I'll pop round tomorrow then, Maria," said Fiona, "About eleven o'clock."

They all made their way downstairs to the front door, just in time to see Mr Johnson's Land Rover sweeping into the drive. William opened the door and a flurry of snowflakes entered the hallway. It was pitch black now outside although the snow gave off a luminous glow. It positively glistened where it caught in the Land Rover's headlights and William noticed that the branches of the fir trees to his right were already starting to sag under the weight of the snow that had landed there.

"This looks like it's here to stay for a while." William shouted over to Mr Johnson.

"Aye, that it does… and you can bet the whole bloomin' country'll come grinding to a halt!" he shouted back.

After a few minutes conversation with the kind of camaraderie that adverse weather conditions invariable brings, Fiona and Mr Johnson set off for home in their respective four wheel drives and Maria, William and Emily headed for the warmth of their front room. William wondered if the gritter lorries would have cleared the roads before he was due to set off for work the next morning. Emily wondered about the best place in the garden to build a snowman. And Maria wondered how she was ever going to survive tomorrow's task of picking over and packing up Bobby's favourite clothes and prized possessions.

Chapter 15

WHEN EMILY AWOKE THE NEXT MORNING and looked out of her bedroom window it was obvious that yet more snow had fallen during the night. William now had the task of digging his car out of a snowdrift at the front of the house which he said he'd do after walking Emily the short journey to school. He was surprised that she hadn't used the severe snow conditions as an excuse for not going to school but then she reminded him she had good reason for wanting to attend… it was a rehearsal day for the school's Christmas concert and Emily's class was performing the story of The Little Matchstick Girl. Emily had been chosen by the class teacher to play the lead role and she was thoroughly enjoying the fuss and attention that came with it. As it turned out there was hardly any audience to speak of that day… so many children and a fair proportion of the staff had called in to say they were snowbound that the decision was made to close the school at lunchtime. The novelty of the situation almost made up for the non-rehearsal of the play and Emily crunched home through the snow with specific plans to build a quite huge snowman in the middle of the back lawn. She called in at the newsagents on the way home to buy a packet of opal fruits and a sherbet fountain. Abba's Money, Money, Money was playing on a transistor radio plugged in behind the counter, and Mrs Porter who owned the shop joked that it was so true – couldn't they all do with a little money, money money?

When she eventually arrived home the song was playing on a different radio station, and Emily never heard it again without being instantly transported to that snowy week back in December 1976. Maria, who had opened the front door to let Emily in was now wondering how she would react to the sight of the chaos in Bobby's room and the few packed boxes waiting on the landing to be put up into the loft. Emily said an awkward 'hello' to Fiona who looked guilty at being caught with a handful of Bobby's vests, before going into her own room to get changed out of her school uniform. In fact Emily didn't stop busying herself with thick socks, boots, gloves and a handful of biscuits until she came to a halt at the bottom of the garden. *What was mum doing with Bobby's things?* Why did anything have to be done with them? Why couldn't the door just be shut on that room so the memory of Bobby and everything he owned could be locked away and kept forever? Lock it all away so it couldn't hurt. Why did anything have to change? *Why, why, why?*

With a surge of energy born of frustration and fear she stooped down and moulded a ball from a handful of snow. Then she rolled it along, yard after yard, around the garden and back and forth, never stopping, never slowing down, until eventually she was wrestling with a ball of snow so big she could hardly push it forward another inch. Out of breath and physically drained she stopped… and felt her eyes drawn to the one place she didn't want to look at – the first floor window of Bobby's room. The curtains twitched as Maria made to move away, and then realising that Emily had seen her she stopped and gave a cheery wave.

By the time darkness fell late that afternoon, Bobby's room had been stripped bare and a robust snowman stared back at the house from the middle of the lawn. Maria's face was pinched and drawn as she shivered on the back doorstep admiring Emily's handiwork. Oh, to be a snowman with a heart of ice and the ability to melt away when the going got tough. What a shitty day it had been. What a heartbreaking job she had done, methodically, mechanically going through Bobby's things, shoving them up in the loft because she could bare to neither keep them nor give them away. And even the loft itself had spewed forth another agony which would have to be faced over the next week – the Christmas decorations. Why had they always made such a big deal of decorating the house, turned the putting up of the tree and the decorations into such a momentous occasion? They'd built it up into such an important family event that now, this year, it would rate extremely highly on that list of painful 'firsts'. William half solved the problem by taking Emily on a shopping trip to Dawson's to buy a complete set of new decorations. The old set, with their faults and quirks and endearing shabbiness would now be forever consigned to the loft, to be replaced by a new set; bright, shiny and unfamiliar - straight from the shop display with not a hint of family Christmases gone by.

But although new decorations could be bought and the tree could be positioned in a different part of the room this year, the fact remained that Christmas day itself could not be changed. Emily continued to push away all thoughts of Bobby and the Christmas he would be missing and threw herself wholeheartedly into her role as the matchstick girl. William went through the motions of going to work every day and Maria floated through the run up to Christmas day like a zombie, not bothering to write cards and not caring if the presents she bought were suitable for their recipients or not. The 25th December loomed ahead like some monstrous beast, glaring out of the calendar page like a giant beacon, dwarfing the dates surrounding it, making them pale into insignificance. The 25th December – a date that demands perfection in all aspects of domesticity; perfectly wrapped presents and roaring fires, fresh coffee and juicy Satsumas, and a tree which has resisted its natural instinct to shed most of its needles. Festive fun and goodwill to all men. This is what Christmas day demands but rarely ever gets. In previous years, the inner circle of relations and friends had traditionally come to Maria and William on Christmas evening. This meant they could have the whole pyjama-clad day to themselves before a mad tidy up at about five o'clock. Then Maria would make a buffet spread and they would all change into their party clothes in time for the onslaught of in-laws, aunts and uncles at seven. Maria had balked at the idea of having everyone over this year and so William had subtly put about the word that they would, quite understandably, be having a quiet

Christmas on their own. Personally he thought it was a big mistake to be left to their own devises and thoughts on such a poignant day and was relieved when Maria bowed to the pressure of Fiona's invite to spend the evening with her and her husband, Neil.

As far as Emily was concerned it was a completely different little girl who walked down the stairs on Christmas day morning compared to the same time last year. The child was gone. The child and the childishness and the giggling and the unreserved enthusiasm had gone and Emily walked into the front room and sat on the edge of the settee in the same polite manner as an adult might do. The silence was deafening until William, with false gusto, made a meal of turning on the television and flicking through the channels in order to bring some Christmas noise into the house. Maria padded in in her dressing gown and gave Emily a hug. No amount of cold water and Ponds day cream could hide the fact that she had been crying. Her eye lids were raw and swollen and the skin on her cheeks wore the kind of tell tale blotches that only a prolonged bout of acute sobbing can bring. Emily felt guilty for wanting to tear into her pile of presents and so sat there restrained, watching the St Luke's Church Choir give its rendition of While Shepherds Watched Their Flocks By Night. When coffee had been made and toast and cereal dutifully swallowed the opening of the presents began. 'Oohs' and 'ahs' were said in all the appropriate places and presents to each other were given with pleasure and received with thanks, no one wanting to break the fragile balance of calm acceptance that had descended on the morning.

After Christmas lunch, which Maria had put together with robotic precision, Emily settled down to watch Christmas Top of the Pops. Maria went upstairs to lie down and William announced that he was going for a walk. In just a few seconds the family had dispersed; a far cry from the usual Christmas afternoon when they would all watch the TV together, passing comment on the chart hits of the year and eating endless amounts of Milk Tray and Quality Street.

William set off down the road, heading nowhere in particular but finding himself trudging towards Whitemoor Farm. Emily always seemed to find sanctuary in the place and maybe he would too. Christ, it was exhausting, draining… just the effort of putting one foot in front of the other day in day out left him feeling physically weak. It was such a strain trying to keep spirits up, trying to stay positive, stay focused, lest the family he had left should implode and simply vanish in the aftermath. He kicked away a large stone which had found its way onto the lane and in doing so fired a spray of slush into the air. The Christmas card snow had not lasted until Christmas day and all that was left was a dreary wet slush in the roads and the grey stumpy remains of snowmen in gardens and fields. William breathed the cold, dry winter air deep into his lungs and felt glad and sad at the same time that he had been able to escape the house for an hour to be on his own. What a great fuss we all make about Christmas he thought, yet here it was, nothing more than a cold, grey and miserable winter's day just like countless others. Just because it was Christmas day what did people expect? Carol singers on every corner? Santa and Rudolph flying about overhead? Streamers and balloons and a bloody hourly fanfare? William shook his head and opened the gate into the stable yard. Mr Johnson was walking across it with a wheel barrow.

"Oh, hello Mr West. Merry Christmas to you! You haven't come down to see to Rascal have you, 'cos I told Emily to leave all that to me over Christmas."

"No… just taking a walk to work off some of that Christmas pudding and I found myself heading for here…"

"Aye well, go and say hello to the horses then and I'll tell Mrs Johnson to put the kettle on… better still, I bet you could manage a brandy with us, eh?"

William agreed and as he gazed down the field to the horses at the bottom he began to understand why Emily found this simple, rustic place such a marvellous one to escape to. And by the time he set off for home again, warmed and settled by the brandy, he knew that the three of them would get through this bloody year, see it through to the very end… If Christmas day had been a monumental effort to get through then New Year's Eve promised to be even more so. And beyond that? Well, who knew what lay ahead, but they *would* survive. For Emily's sake they'd bloody well have to.

Chapter 16

On New Year's Eve that year Darren O'Dowel was working. His employers, Radio City, were doing a live broadcast from a popular night club and it was down to the engineering department to set up the feed so that the revelry happening at 'Maxim's' could be played out in all its glory to the local audience. The party was being broadcast between eleven and one but the engineering department was at the club by eight o'clock in order to sort out the technicalities of such a venture. There was already a steady trickle of party goers coming through the doors, all of them determined to drink too much, dance too vigorously and laugh too loudly – for this was New Year's Eve, a party night for amateurs, where even the most timid and reserved felt obliged to bellow out the countdown to midnight and dance on 'til dawn.

By ten o'clock Darren was happy that the live broadcast would start an hour later without any hitches and he sat down in a dark corner behind the record decks to drink his beer and survey the scene. In front of him the house DJ was lording it over the several hundred people gyrating on the dance floor, encouraging them to 'get down on it' and 'do it madly at Maxim's'. Do it fucking *badly* more like thought Darren, thinking that the dickhead DJ in front of him was possibly even more of a dickhead DJ than the one who would be turning up from Radio City

The End of Emily West

to do the live show. Christ, these people who apparently made a half decent living by spinning discs couldn't have a brain between them! All they had was a microphone and a big mouth that worked faster than the speed of light. That and an ego the size of a small planet.

The music thumped on relentlessly, an endless beat of pop music sewn together effortlessly by the DJ – so much so that it was almost impossible to pinpoint where one song ended and the next one began. Darren finished his beer and fought his way outside to the engineering van which was parked at the back of the club. Sitting in the driver's seat he fished out the half bottle of whiskey he'd stashed in the glove box. The golden liquid burnt his throat as he tipped his head back with a sigh. Closing his eyes he thought idly over the events of the past year. Freedom from Davina, that's what 1976 had brought him and thank Christ she hadn't kicked up a fuss about that broken cheekbone. She'd let several weeks go by before enlightening him about the extent of the injury he'd inflicted and had sent two further letters asking for him to consider a reconciliation. Darren had almost laughed out loud at that idea... she might get a goodbye fuck if she was lucky when she called round to collect the last of her things from the house... A loud knock on the window made him nearly jump out of his skin.

"What the *frig*..."

"Sorry Darren," chirped the offender as she opened the van door. "Mel Green, trainee news reporter at our beloved Radio City! I'm putting together a New Year's Eve report for the morning show tomorrow. Fancy giving me an interview?"

"You must be frigging joking!" he replied, although she seemed so cocksure of herself that Darren couldn't be too certain.

"Ha! Nearly had you there! Seriously though, I though I'd come and find sanctuary with the engineering department seeing as it's turning into hell on earth inside the club. It's so *hot* in there. Anyway, John's just arrived and he's getting the jitters about his first live link at eleven. I think he wants you to come in and hold his hand. Can I smell whiskey by the way? Go on then, Daz, give us a swig!"

Darren's thoughts of a goodbye fuck with Davina now turned sharply to thoughts of a hello fuck with Mel. Life was definitely better when you were a free agent. Still, if she twittered on like this in bed he'd have to gag her… now there was a thought….

"I can assure you I'd rather be holding your hand than John's," he said, giving Mel the benefit of a long, black-eyed stare. And with that a giggling Mel led a very happy Darren back into the melting pot of Maxim's.

At ten minutes to midnight the DJ had successfully managed to whip up the crowd into a frenzy of New Year excitement. Bodies throbbed and sweated on the dance floor as the magical hour of midnight grew ever closer. Mel had gone back to the van to get a fresh tape and Darren was in a small space between the record decks and the dance floor checking on a loose wire connection underneath the console. A tug at his shirt sleeve made him stand up and turn around, but instead of the flirtatious Mel he was confronted with a drunk and stoned Davina Bailey.

"Happy New Year, happy husband," she shouted, her words fighting with the music. Then she staggered slightly and fell against him.

"I want to talk to you Darren… I want to talk to you *right now*…"

The last few words were screamed and then she made to get down on her knees, shouting, "I'll beg you if I have to!"

"For fuck's sake," said Darren, scarcely able to hold his temper in the very public surroundings, "At least let's get outside you stupid little *cow*."

Darren led her by his well trodden back route to the outside of the night club. He pushed her back roughly up against the breeze block wall, his fast breathing mixing with the sound of her tears and the now muffled sound of the disco.

"Stop fucking crying, can't you?" he raged.

"I knew you'd be here, Darren," Davina started, her earlier confidence sucked out of her by the bitter cold air and Darren's rough handling. "I'm your wife! I'm still your wife and I want us to try again. I'll do anything you want me to, Darren. I'm *begging* you, just give me another chance…"

Darren cut her short. "You've got no fucking pride, have you? And no fucking sense. You know what my New Year's resolution is going to be, eh? To get a divorce from you as soon as friggin' possible. Get that into your thick head!"

Then they both turned as Mel's chirpy little voice shouted over, "Got the new tape Darren… see you inside then. Don't miss the countdown will you?!"

"Who the fuck is that?" screamed Davina as Mel hurried away.

"Someone who's a lot fucking brighter than you are," Darren replied, leaving a shell shocked Davina to slide down the wall to the gravely floor, just in time to hear cries of 'ten, nine, eight, seven,' from the heat and happiness of the night club dance floor.

By twenty minutes past midnight Davina was at a friend's house where she knew she would find a hypodermic needle. By half past she was injecting herself in the arm with weed killer. And by twenty minutes to one o'clock on New's Day, Davina Bailey was dead.

Darren's parents, Elsa and Albert, saw in the New Year at a dinner dance held at the local town hall. Albert looked around at the sagging bunting, the lack lustre bunches of balloons and the jazz band members who were now tired and somewhat red in the face. An oak panelled function room in a high class hotel would have been more to his liking but no one had invited them to such an event and the price of celebrating at that kind of establishment off their own backs made it unattainable. Elsa seemed to be enjoying herself however, much to Albert's annoyance. In fact he had quite wanted to reach over and slap her across her silly face when she had gushed on about how *delicious* the food was. Albert came to the conclusion that his poor, deluded wife wouldn't know fine food it if rammed itself down her throat. Albert checked his watch and loosened his collar. How long now before they could escape this shallow evening of utter boredom? He drank three large mouthfuls of brandy in quick succession. Rammed. Down her throat. Christ, it didn't take much to bring back the memories of that night all those years ago… that night when Darren had exposed his mother as a cheating whore and Albert had been forced to drag her upstairs and teach her a lesson. He'd broken Elsa that night. Crushed her spirit in such a way that it brought him a strange physical pleasure just thinking about it. She'd been submissive and compliant ever since then – a faithful wife and a willing servant – totally obedient as only a good wife should be.

Elsa walked over to Albert then with a glass of wine for each of them. The countdown to midnight was not too far away.

"Any New Year's resolutions, Albert?" she asked him meekly.

"Yes," he replied as he leered towards her, "To ram it down your throat more often. "

The jaded band struck up a new tune and Albert drank his wine greedily, not even bothering to wipe it away as dribbled down his chin.

Barbara Ellery sat quietly in the living room of the house in Brighton which was owned by her sister. Margaret came into the room carrying a tray with two glasses of dry sherry and several slices of Christmas cake.

"What a to do outside, Barbara! Go and look out of the window!"

Barbara dutifully did as she was told and went over to the bay window. Seaside towns work like magnets to party goers on New Year's Eve, she thought, and she watched as the brave and the foolhardy tripped and stumbled over the rocks, drinking, shouting and swearing and playing 'chicken' with the waves. It was bitterly cold outside due in no small part to the high wind that had whipped up around the coast line. The young don't feel the cold though Barbara, and she gave an involuntary shiver despite Margaret having turned on three bars of the electric fire. She looked out beyond the beach and the crashing waves towards the vast black ocean. What was on the horizon? What was out there? The blackness of the sky met the blackness of the water so it was impossible to tell. It rather mirrors my own life thought Barbara, gazing out into the dark, not being able to see anything beyond a wall of black.

"Snap out of it, Barbs!" her sister said crisply as she bustled around the room plumping up cushions. "It's nearly the New Year and it's time for you to start taking control of your life again. I know how it affected you with that poor little boy passing away in the summer – God rest his soul – but really you've been moping about now for far too long."

"I'd got plans to travel…" started Eileen.

"Travel my eye! Get back to what you do best, my dear. Get back in there and teach!"

Barbara heard the clock strike twelve. She took a small sip of dry sherry and for the first time in ages she felt a vague sense of hope.

Emily's friend, Paul Andrew, had been allowed to stay up until midnight but the truth was he could barely keep his eyes open. His ears were open though and lying back on the sofa he could hear quite clearly his mum and dad chatting about the year that had been and the year that was about to come.

"Not a bad year, all told…" said his dad as he poured himself another beer.

"I'd say we've had a really good year, love… I mean to say, when you compare it to what the West's have been through… doesn't bare thinking about…"

"Come on now," said dad, suddenly upbeat and animated, "I'm not having sad thoughts on New Year's Eve. It's nearly midnight… so roll on 1977! And if all goes to plan we could be seeing in the eighties in Sydney – how about that?"

Paul's mum and dad clinked their glasses together with a 'cheers' and a kiss. Sydney, Australia! Paul had heard them speak of their plans to emigrate 'down under' many times. Better job prospects for his dad… not to mention the sun, the sand, the sea. He'd been excited at first until he'd heard it discussed so often it had lost its initial sense of magic. Whether they would emigrate or whether is was all simply 'talk' was difficult to say. He forced his eyes open, determined to see in the New Year. What he saw instead was a sparkle in his parents' eyes which he hadn't noticed before and when the bells on the television chimed midnight he got a sudden rush of feeling that a move to Sydney, Australia might actually happen after all.

William poured himself a glass of wine from the fridge and wished there was something he could do to lessen Maria's pain.

"I'll have one as well, thanks," she said sitting down at the kitchen table. "Hardly to celebrate, of course… rather to try and knock myself out. That's what I'm going to do between now and midnight – get gloriously drunk!"

"I know love… it's a bloody bad night for us… I know…"

"If I'd have thought earlier," Maria continued recklessly, "I could have got some sleeping tablets and taken them after tea… then I could have slept through this whole miserable New Year's Eve rubbish. In fact, that's what I'll do next year, sleep through it all. Emily was in bed asleep at nine. She had the right idea."

"Yes, maybe…"

William and Maria sat at the kitchen table in silence yet inside Maria's head the shouting and screaming was almost deafening. It was wrong, it was an injustice, it wasn't fair. All the questions, all the inadequate answers and the constant, relentless battering of *why, why, why*? And the awful, bitter knowledge that she could never again take the New Year for granted. 1977 – what would that bring? The cheers, the good wishes, the hopes and plans for the future. How blind. How short-sighted and completely blind. None of it meant anything when you knew it could all be taken away from you. Maria knew that now. How easily the words 'Happy New Year' could be turned into a sick joke. Well, she'd had it with New Year and resolved there and then to never, ever celebrate it again for as long as she lived.

Upstairs, Emily looked at the clock at the side of her bed. The time was midnight. She'd had a restless sleep since nine o'clock but was glad she'd woken to see the defining moment when the two hands on the clock become one. 1977. It was 1977. 1976 was now firmly in the past and 1977 lay before the world like an open book. It was whilst she was thinking about this, staring up at the ceiling that Emily got the curious feeling that she didn't want to be here. Not that she didn't want to be in her bed or in that house but that she actually didn't want to exist. No, that was putting it too strongly… trying hard to make sense of it she came to the conclusion that she might not care whether she existed or not. It was puzzling and unsettling and she was disappointed to find that the next day the feeling of indifference had not gone away.

The Middle

Chapter 17

EMILY FLOPPED DOWN ON HER BED in a hot, exhausted heap and wished once again that the weathermen wouldn't keep harking back to the record breaking summer of 1976. She'd begun to feel stiff and awkward and stifled if the subject came up in her mum's presence… it was as if a cloud had suddenly passed overhead – a dull cloud that prodded the memory of that other sun soaked August all those years ago. After a few minutes she stood up and began to change out of the denim shorts and yellow t-shirt she was wearing. They were dusty and grubby and clung to her skin, testament to the fact that she had spent most of the afternoon down at Whitemoor Farm with Rascal. Emily didn't seem destined to grow anymore than her current height of five feet five inches and hence she didn't look out of place on Rascal's back. And anyway, she loathed those people who sold on ponies they'd grown out of, as if they deserved no more compassion than an outgrown pair of shoes or a car that had too many miles on the clock.

She looked out of her bedroom window towards the lawn below. It was early evening on the second day of the school summer holidays. The first year of the sixth form was over and this time next year she would be sitting her 'A' Levels. Then school and study would be over for good. Last year had been easy - easy and carefree and so much fun -

The End of Emily West

basking in the glory of nine top graded 'O' Levels. Everyone knew that the really hard work started this September and Emily knew that she'd really have to apply herself to the course work if she was going to live up to her mum and dad's natural assumption that she'd do well. The 'O' Levels had been a piece of cake in the end – especially with that extra year to study for them… Emily had been thrown from her friend's horse the weekend before the first exam of the original set. She broke her left leg and fractured her right collarbone, leaving the re-sits in the autumn as the only possibility. When a mystery virus saw her back in bed in September Maria and William agreed with the school that the only sensible option was to take the exams the following summer. It had been a pain but Emily supposed that the top grades had made up for it. She had put in plenty of hours and effort so the first year of the sixth form had seemed like a great opportunity to have a bit of a rest.

She watched her dad potter around the garden, grubbing about in a flower border one minute, inspecting the rampant growth of a climbing rose the next. Maria came out with a bowl of dishwater and poured it over a large fuchsia. She and William stood together for a few moments pointing at a cluster of large white flowers and then stooping down to breathe in their scent. They looked happy, comfortable and totally at ease in each other's company. William said something to Maria which made her laugh and Emily felt confident that the grey cloud that the weather report mention of 1976 had created had now passed. Anyway, she sure as hell wasn't going to dwell on it. Grab life by the throat, live it to the full and sod the consequences! The past was past. Now was now. And a beautiful, lazy summer stretched out before her. It was difficult to say exactly when this 'oh fuck it' attitude had become the religion which Emily lived most of her life by… it had sort of crept upon her, a realisation that she didn't care whether she was on planet Earth or not. There was a certain suppressed bitterness which had been there since Bobby died - a bitterness born of the absolute certainty that there was not a God, that tragedy may strike at any given moment… that writing on the floorboards of the cottage at Woolacombe had just been a pointless, childish game.

Emily walked across to her wardrobe and pondered on what to wear the next day. Tomorrow was the first day of the three day Greenshires County Show, a large agricultural show about ten miles away. The event had been going for a number of years with varying degrees of success; heaving with tourists when the weather was good and little more than a depressing mud bath when the heavens decided to open. The Greenshires Show was much like any other annual agricultural show in content; show jumping and sheep dog displays, falconry and master classes in the art of dry stone walling... country pursuits in one show ring whilst in a marquee next door people from all over the place came to sell their arts and crafts or antiques and bric-a-brac. Further exploration would reveal a fast-food village, a large beer tent and a stage for a local band, and from here a trail of cold chips mashed into the grass would lead to a fun fair; a bright and brash array of white knuckle rides, lucky dips and candy floss.

There was something new on the agenda however at this year's Greenshires County Show. A local poster campaign was promoting the fact that the area's new commercial radio station 'Rocket Sound' was broadcasting some of its shows live from the showground. Rocket Sound had taken to the airwaves some six months ago with a huge amount of local publicity. If fans of the station wanted to meet the faces behind the voices and maybe get a free car sticker or baseball hat, now was their chance. Emily was going to the show on the bus with her friend from school, Jackie Dean. Maria was accompanying William on a business lunch at a nearby country hotel and had offered to collect them both from the showground in the evening.

An inspection of the contents of the wardrobe offered up some interesting possibilities but it was a pair of white jeans and a souvenir t-shirt of one of The Jam's last ever tours which were laid out on the chair ready to be put on the next day. Emily stared at it... the navy blue T-shirt with the turquoise writing... the t-shirt she kept for special occasions and always wore with such love and pride... the t-shirt that upon seeing it instantly brought back such bitter-sweet memories that for one moment she would be tempted to fold it up and put it at the back of a little used drawer, never to see the light of day again.

The End of Emily West

The year that Emily discovered The Jam, and discovered what it was to be utterly smitten with a pop band and their music, was the same year that she lost them. It was also the year that Karen Black and her family moved to Bristol and that Paul Andrew's parents finally did what they'd always been threatening – moved their family to Sydney, Australia. 1982... God, it was only last year. What a lot had happened and how fast the time had passed. Last year... she had only watched The Jam on Top of the Pops that night in February because there was such a fuss going on about their single which had gone straight into the charts at number one – a rare and phenomenal feat. Heather had come bounding into the classroom that day saying her elder brother had been pounding the air with excitement over it and by the end of the day Heather had single-handedly managed to whip up the whole class into a great frenzy of anticipation over that evening's edition of Top of the Pops. When Emily saw The Jam perform A Town Called Malice she suddenly had no idea why she'd never clued onto this group before. They were unique, angry and passionate and in so being had immediately given Emily an ally – a glamorous, passionate ally she could swear allegiance to and worship forever. Looking up from her magazine Maria had commented, "Well, at least they look smart in those suits..." Amazing! Even her mum had been impressed by them to some degree, which made the begging of pocket money to go and buy current and past albums somewhat easier.

Emily's enthusiasm for the group had quickly rubbed off on her best friend Karen Black and the two of them would talk endlessly about the merits of one song over another and confide in each other about their dreams of somehow meeting the three band members and being whisked away to a life of parties and recording studios. All other groups paled into insignificance at that time and indeed the likes of Duran Duran and Harircut 100 were to be pitied and sneered at for their pretty boy looks and lightweight lyrics. So, when Emily and Karen found out that their next tour included a venue just some forty minutes away from them, there was no question about it – they had to go. Unfortunately William and Maria visibly balked at the sight of the ticket Emily had bought from a local record shop and it took days of begging and pleading, tears and tantrums for them to agree that she could go, and that was on the strict understanding that William and Maria would drive her and Karen there and wait in the car until the concert was over. The decision of what to wear then was an easy one as it didn't really matter what was worn as long as the obligatory parka, the most essential park of the Mod uniform, was kept on at all times. Maria hated the scruffy green coat with its tatty fake fur trim around the hood and she didn't think much of the Union Jack with The Jam written on it which Emily insisted on sewing onto the back. When she thought back to how her little girl used to dress; skirts and dresses and pretty in pink… well, thank God other mothers had assured her that this was just a phase her daughter would eventually grow out of. And had she really heard correctly that one of those Jam songs had said 'fucking' somewhere in one of the verses? Yet there was little point in asking Emily about it because she would only go off into a big sulk and Maria couldn't stand any more strops and stamping of feet. Really, the end of this 'phase' couldn't come a moment too soon!

When the dream came true and William and Maria dropped them off as near to The Duke Hall as they could get the girls jostled and pushed their way into the concert building. Emily thought how weird it was to see so many like minded fans all in the one place. What claim did these other people have on the band when obviously she and Karen were their most loyal followers? Fans eyed each other up warily and most were older than Emily and Karen. But with all the confidence and recklessness of youth and the cocoon-like security of the parka coats the pair held their own, pushing their way to the front with chins in the air and not a care for anything or anyone else.

Looking back now the concert seemed more like a hazy dream than an event which had actually happened. *'Paul, Bruce, Rick!'* Girls screaming in an effort to get themselves just one second's eye contact with their heroes… the smell of young sweaty bodies and stale cigarette smoke… spilt drinks, more pushing, more shoving and the surreal vision of the people you idolised actually physically there on the stage – a few yards away but ultimately worlds apart. Before the end Emily and Karen went over to the merchandise stand wishing they had enough money to buy one of everything on offer. As it was they settled for a tour t-shirt each. 'A Solid Bond In Your Heart' the t-shirt proclaimed on the front and it went on to list all the dates and venues for the 'Solid Bond Tour' on the back. On the back seat of the car the girls spent the journey home in a daze – dazed for the fact that they had had an unbelievably brilliant time and dazed for the fact that this was obviously not the night that The Jam were going to pluck them from the crowd and transport them to their new life. But such was the belief that this would surely one day happen that by the following morning Emily and Karen weren't unduly worried… there were years ahead of them weren't there? Years of new singles and new albums, new tours and new opportunities to meet the band and for their lives to change forever… years of wishing, hoping and dreaming….

But just a few weeks later came the most cruel and vicious of blows - The Jam had decided to spilt up. Heather came into school one morning brandishing that week's copy of Smash Hits. *'The Jam throw in the towel!'* screamed the front page headline. Emily snatched it off her and read the story in stunned disbelief. This just wasn't happening… it wasn't possible that Paul, Bruce and Rick had agreed to go their separate ways, that Paul in particular had decided to head off in a new direction… they were The Jam for fuck's sake… they were meant to be together forever…. Karen Black started to cry and Heather tried to comfort her. Emily quietly handed her back the magazine and wondered if life without The Jam was even worth living. A good number of pupils didn't take in much of what was being taught in school that day. The Jam was splitting up, and the hopes and dreams of a generation came crashing to the ground.

So, Emily's and Karen's heady few months of musical paradise had come to an end and as if to compound the tide of change it brought about Karen broke the news to Emily of her family's imminent move to Bristol. Her father's firm was relocating there and they were to move by the start of the new school term in the autumn. Emily and Karen swore to keep in touch, swore to always be the best of friends and swore to be true fans of The Jam forever. They even dared to hope that the band would change their minds, that Paul would realise the stupidity of his actions and keep the band together after all. They weren't splitting up until the end of the year so there was still hope, wasn't there? But it seemed like the black clouds were brewing that autumn for no sooner had Karen departed than Paul Andrew told Emily of his family's plans to finally make the break and move to Australia. Over the last few years Emily and Paul had become close and were therefore both rather upset at this new turn of events. Paul swore to return when he was older and could do as he liked. They both swore to write and 'phone and keep in touch, but like Karen before him Paul was making pacts and promises with Emily which were destined to be broken.

It was fortunate timing for Emily that a new girl came into her class in the first term of the New Year. Jackie Dean was another victim of a job promotion and relocation and did little more than sulk for her first few weeks at her new school. Emily did her best to chip away at Jackie's iron clad exterior and in no time at all they'd become joined at the hip, due in no small part to the fact that Jackie had a parka coat and was not only an authority on The Jam but also The Who and The Kinks. It was also an attraction that Jackie had actually already slept with a boy – gone all the way, actually had *sex* – whereas Emily had only ever kissed Paul and could hardly imagine what it must be like to actually *sleep* with someone. Doubtless in time Jackie could enlighten her in graphic detail.

Emily draped the white jeans and Jam t-shirt over the back of her dressing table chair ready for the morning and thought about Jackie's promiscuous and flirtatious nature which was becoming increasingly infectious. Whereas a year ago Emily wouldn't have dared to be as overtly brash and brazen as her friend, she now found that she longed for the excitement and adventure that always seemed to be coming Jackie's way. Surely a move to some big city would provide all that and more? Her master plan was to go to university or some kind of college in London. She really had no idea what kind of career she wanted from such a move. In fact all she knew for sure was that London was definitely the place to be. Several day trips with Maria to the capital over the years had convinced Emily of this and she was hell bent on experiencing all the glitz and glamour that the big city would undoubtedly offer. Of course being of the age where reality and practicalities are not worth even the briefest of consideration, Emily had not got beyond the rather hazy vision of regular visits to the Harrods Food Halls, picnics in St James' Park, shopping in Carnaby Street and boat trips down the River Thames; all this to escape to and find... something to live for.

Chapter 18

SITTING AT THE BACK OF THE bus the next morning Emily and Jackie took out compact mirrors and applied extra layers of lipstick that was simply not needed. Jackie brushed on another layer of mascara for good measure and then cast a critical eye over her arms, wishing that the fake tan she'd put on the night before hadn't streaked quite so badly.

"Planning to do any school stuff over the holidays?" she asked Emily.

"No way! I don't intend to even *open* a book until we go back to school. I mean, what are the holidays for? They're to relax and have fun, that's what they're for… unless you're Joanne Cooper of course. Bloody swot!"

Jackie giggled, "God, yes! She gets on my tits, she really does. If she gets less than seventy percent in anything she thinks she's done really badly. And that hair! With a good cut and a bit of make-up she could look totally different…"

"Yeah, but she'd still be a bloody swot."

"Here," began Jackie, rummaging around in her bag, "Fancy a John Player Black?" And she casually handed Emily an opened packet of cigarettes.

"Oh my *God*! How long have you had those? How many have you had?"

"I haven't had any yet. I was waiting for you!" That infectious giggle again. "I bought a lighter too… and some strong mints for afterwards…."

Emily and Jackie lit two cigarettes and actually did little more than hold them and occasionally put their lips to the filter.

"How do you inhale?" asked Emily.

"Haven't a clue… I think you've just got to practice… actually I think you have to sort of suck and swallow at the same time…"

The two girls looked at each other and bust into fits of raucous laughter at the obvious double meaning of the last comment. An elderly lady about half way down the bus turned around to give them a disapproving look. Emily saw the look but didn't care. She didn't care about anything. The sun was shining and she was free today to do as she pleased. How could she possibly have known it was to be her last day of true freedom for a long, long time.

It was eleven o'clock when they arrived at the Greenshires County Show and they started off their tour of the ground with a look at the bargain clothes stalls. Waxed jackets, embroidered kaftans and floppy straw hats were all here for the taking with 'special show offer' and 'summer bargain' banners enticing shoppers to part with their money. In the midst of all this a fast talking salesman was demonstrating a 'five-in-one' vegetable slicer, the kind of ingenious gadget which works so well for the person who's selling it but refuses to perform when the gullible buyer gets it home. The man kept winking at Emily and Jackie as he reeled out his babble of sales patter and in return Jackie fluttered her mascara laden eyelashes back at him and made a great show of lighting a cigarette in what she assumed was a seductive manner. After they'd watched the Wonder-Slicer magically chop up a carrot for the second time of asking Emily insisted that they head off to the horse rings to watch the showing classes. Jackie stood and humoured the situation for about ten minutes before telling Emily she was off to find the Rocket Sound Roadshow they'd all seen so heavily advertised. Emily wanted to see who won the class she was watching and so agreed to meet Jackie over there.

A dark bay horse cantered around the ring, coming so close to Emily that she could have reached out and touched him. His glossy coat shone like polished mahogany and his rider wore immaculate clothing which could easily have been new on that day. Between them they oozed competence and horsemanship and a glance over to the collecting ring confirmed they weren't the only ones by a long shot to adhere to such high standards. These were the professionals, these people were the true horsemen and women and Emily looked on with a pang of regret that she and Rascal had only ever played at the game and never truly been a part of it. After she'd seen and applauded the judges' decision she followed the map on the back of her souvenir show programme and ambled over to the Rocket Sound Roadshow. Quite a crowd had gathered around the stage as the music blasted out of the speaker towers that stood to either side of it and a station DJ strutted up and down throwing out Rocket Sound car stickers like confetti at a wedding. Jackie ran over to Emily clutching a bunch of them and waving them in her face.

"Hah, get a load of this! They've got a live band coming on soon. Let's hang round here for a bit!"

"Yeah, OK then," said Emily and stood there trying to feel cool and trendy in amongst all this madness.

The band came on, a local group called Party House who were just about to release their first single. Jackie lit up another John Player but tempting as it was Emily refused, terrified of being seen by someone who knew her and would pass on the scandalous news to her parents. They'd kill her if they ever caught her with a cigarette. She may as well be injecting heroin for all the upset it would cause. She surveyed the scene before them. Great patches of sweat stained the underarms of the t-shirt worn by the lead singer as he put his heart and soul into an enthusiastic rendition of the forthcoming single. Even at this pre-famous stage of their career young girls were lurching forward to try and grab the singer's trouser legs and someone in a Rocket Sound t-shirt had to stop a freckle-faced girl of about thirteen from knocking him off his feet altogether. The Rocket Sound Roadshow consisted of a large black trailer which converted into a stage, a stall which sold all manor of novelties bearing the Rocket Sound logo and a black van with a huge radio mast soaring up from its roof. The black paintwork of the vehicles was plastered with the Rocket Sound logo, a graphic which portrayed, predictably, a rocket – bright red in colour with a splash of gold depicting the after burn. The slogan, *'Gets You To The Stars'* wooshed away with the upward thrust of the spacecraft and all in all it was the kind of sleek, showbiz spectacle that people of the local area simply hadn't witnessed before.

Emily headed off to get two trays of chips from a nearby chip van and she and Jackie spent the next hour sitting on the grass observing the Rocket Sound Roadshow and soaking up the sun. The air was ripe with the smell of fast food and hot horses, and the intense aroma of Jackie's cigarette smoke drifted around their heads.

"God, I need a drink!" said Jackie suddenly.

Jackie said things like that, things which would have been better suited coming from the mouth of someone some ten years her senior, for there was no chance she was expressing a sudden desire for lemonade or orange juice.

"Me too!" agreed Emily and they sauntered off to the beer tent. With their two plastic half pint glasses slopping over with creamy froth they escaped the greenhouse of a tent and quickly laid claim to a suddenly vacant outdoor table featuring four rickety wooden chairs and a tatty parasol.

"Hey, this is the life," quipped Emily, smacking her lips together and wiping the froth from them with the back of her hand.

"Oh, that's charming!" said a man's voice beside her. "Mind if I sit here?" And he'd sat down before either Emily or Jackie could agree or object.

Emily felt ruffled by the intrusion of this dark-eyed, over confident stranger but Jackie regained her composure almost immediately.

"Well, it's a free country," she said sarcastically, and rummaged in her bag for her rapidly depleting supply of John Player cigarettes.

"So," said the man, "What brings you two ladies here today?"

Jackie quickly summed him up as a smug prick but hoped he might offer to buy them another drink.

"Oh, we're just having a day out," Emily replied politely.

"Great… and what are your names?"

"I'm Jackie," said Jackie, blowing a mouthful of smoke in the man's face.

"Christ, what are you trying to do, set me on fire?"

Emily giggled and drained the last dregs of beer from her glass.

"And I'm Emily," she said, "Emily West."

"Well, pleased to meet you Jackie and Emily. Would you like another beer? Good, I'll get them in. My name's Darren, by the way… Darren O'Dowel."

Chapter 19

WHEN DARREN O'DOWEL SPOTTED THE VACANT chair at the table occupied by two nubile young ladies he thought he may as well avail himself of it. It was that or the spare stool next to the overweight man and his panting hairy dog. Darren couldn't quite place the girls' ages – twenty maybe? - so he was surprised to discover they were still teenagers and still at school. The one called Jackie was a right hard-faced cow but the blonde one, Emily, now she was quite a different proposition altogether. Darren bought them two further beers and sat back in amusement as their tongues got looser and their voices grew louder. Even the blonde was puffing away at the cigarettes now and as she started going into great detail about some Jam concert she'd been to once he wondered idly if she was a virgin. Over the next boozy hour he told them all about his job as Chief Engineer at Rocket Sound and he could tell that he'd suddenly gone up in their estimation. To most people 'radio' equalled 'famous people and a glamorous showbiz life' and he could tell that these two were no different. Oh well, it wasn't the first time he'd capitalised on this assumption although he could do with loosing Jackie in the crowd. Emily was almost too good to be true; fifteen years his junior, blonde yet bright, innocent yet forthright. Still, Jackie was obviously here for the duration so he decided to put up with her until he could ask Emily out on her own.

Eventually Darren said his break was over and he had to get back to the Roadshow in time to set up the live link back to the studio at three o'clock. He invited Emily and Jackie to come back with him so he could show them what went on backstage and introduce them to some of the people who worked at Rocket.

"Rocket Sound!" Emily said in a sing song voice, "Gets You To The Stars!"

"Yeah," said Darren, "Or as we all like to say, "Gets You Up The Arse!"

And the two girls trailed behind him in fits of giggles.

By the end of the day Emily and Darren had swapped telephone numbers and both girls had agreed with the Promotions Manager to spend two hours selling Rocket Sound merchandise at the next Roadshow in a week's time. It was a week filled with listening to music at home and strolling back and forth to Whitemoor Farm so Emily had more than enough time to think about Darren O'Dowel and the possibility of getting involved with him any further. He was thirty three. There was fifteen years between them…. Not that he looked like some kind of father figure, far from it and from Emily's point of view a man in his thirties could only serve to heighten her levels of maturity and sophistication. His clothes were quite trendy she'd noticed and she'd also liked the look of the silver Ford Sierra he'd parked behind the Roadshow stage. If she really thought about it she didn't fancy *him* as such, more the excitement that he represented. He offered the opportunity for her to go out with a man rather than a boy. He had a great job in a glamorous industry, money, influence and a company car. She could instantly transport herself into a grown up world of candlelit dinners, company parties and gin and tonics. Even thoughts of getting to London were put on hold when she imagined Darren O'Dowel as her ticket to more exciting and meaningful existence.

Of course Emily instinctively knew that her parents would disapprove of a such a relationship so immediately a barrier of her own making went up between them – subtle at first and then a solid wall of resentment as the summer went on and she dared not reveal that she was seeing a man who was so much older than her. After that first meeting at the Greenshires Show Emily became secretive and snappy, her only interests being to escape either to Whitemoor Farm or to Darren and his endless supply of whiskey and ginger ale and Marlborough Lights cigarettes. Maria was both hurt and irritated by the change in her daughter and inevitably her exasperation spilt over and her patience ran out.

"Where are you off to?" Maria asked as Emily came down the stairs one evening in high heels and an outfit she'd obviously taken great care over.

"Just out with Jackie and a few others," she lied, not looking Maria in the eye and almost brushing past her on the bottom step. "Dad said I could take the car."

"Oh, did he indeed?!"

"Why?" Emily challenged, "Is that a problem?"

Maria felt the blood almost fizz inside her head. "The problem, Emily, is you. I don't know what's got into you lately but you can cut it out right now! Your father and I have both noticed it… you've been rude, argumentative, inconsiderate…"

"Oh, for God's sake…"

Maria's eyes were glazing over and she felt almost breathless with anger and frustration. For all the world she could have reached forward and struck her daughter simply to release her own pain which was welling up inside.

"*If only Bobby was still here!*" screamed Maria,

The words hung in the air as Maria's hands flew up to her tear streaked face and Emily ran past her out of the house.

After two miles Emily's stiffened shoulders and tightly set jaw relaxed and she felt the pin prick of tears stabbing at her eyes. All the pain of Bobby's death and all the memories of Bobby's young life had been so easy to block out as a child… nowadays however, as she approached adulthood they were becoming increasingly difficult to suppress. At any given moment random thoughts about her baby brother would bubble to the surface, demanding attention and consideration, demanding to be dissected and analysed. Bobby was increasingly in her thoughts… what would he look like now, had he lived? What would they talk about? Would he love football, scouts, riding Rascal? And would he still adore his older sister as she would still adore him? The questions always threatened to choke her and had to be stuffed quickly back into their box again. Then the overwhelming urge to escape to a different life would envelop her, a warm blanket of temptation which she was only too happy to succumb to.

Eventually the decision about when the right time would be to tell her parents about Darren was taken out of her hands. Towards the end of the summer holidays she went to the cinema with Darren one Saturday night having told Maria and William she was going to a nightclub with Jackie and some other friends from school. The truth of the matter was revealed to Maria by her friend Fiona over lunch the following Wednesday. Ignorant of the situation Fiona spoke quite freely about the fact that she had seen Emily and 'an older man' at the cinema but they'd disappeared into the crowds before she could reach them to say hello. That night a tight lipped and grim faced William asked Emily to sit down for a few minutes so they could talk to her.

"I'm not going to beat about the bush with this, Emily," he said, "But the fact is Fiona saw you at the cinema on Saturday night when you'd definitely told us you were going out somewhere else with your friends from school. She also said that this chap you were with was clearly older than you…. Now, it's not the fact that we don't want you to go out with people, have a boyfriend, of course not… but we'd quite like to know who this man is you're seeing and why you've been deliberately lying to us about it. No! Don't give me that look like I was born yesterday. You've obviously taken up with someone unsuitable or you wouldn't be trying to hide it from us, would you?"

Emily squirmed on the edge of the settee and in a failed attempt at bravado muttered and stumbled her way through the fact that Darren O'Dowel was the thirty three year old Chief Engineer at Rocket Sound and yes, they had been seeing each other.

"Well, I can't say I'm at all happy with this," began William.

"Hah, that's an understatement!" Maria shouted.

"He's a man and he's after one thing…" said William.

The End of Emily West

"Oh God!" said Emily with as much courage and sarcasm as she could muster given these embarrassing circumstances, "He's not like that…"

"Don't 'Oh God' me young lady," said Maria turning on her. "And of course he's 'like that'! What would you know about it? He's a red blooded male and sooner or later he'll want to get into your knickers!"

William looked at Maria, acutely uncomfortable at her uncharacteristically coarse outburst.

Nobody spoke and the air was thick with mutual resentment. The pointlessness of existence bore down on Emily – dark oppressive thoughts like storm clouds hanging low on the horizon. Really and truly, what was the point of it all? Why was life so fucking difficult all the time; petty battles, unnecessary embarrassments, a hundred and one ridiculous hurdles to jump over and just as many hoops of fire to jump through. Awkward and angry over the whole miserable confrontation Emily stomped off to her room and put The Jam on the record player. Anger and frustration barked out of the loudspeakers matching Emily's mood exactly. "Why didn't you stay together?" Emily muttered to the vinyl, "Why does everything good have to change?" And when The Gift LP had finished and the stylus went back into its cradle Emily's anger was spent and she fell into a shallow, unsatisfying sleep.

In the kitchen the next morning William and Maria, it appeared, had had a surprising change of heart. In her teenage arrogance Emily thought it was because they had seen the error of their ways and come to their senses. The truth of the matter however, was the Maria and William had already lost one child and did not want to loose their remaining one. Forbidding Emily to see Darren may drive her away, force her out of their lives and make a rift between them which would never be healed. She may go to university and never return, never ring and never write. And as a deflated William had said to Maria the night before, Emily was not a little girl anymore and would have to start learning from her own mistakes.

"If you're going to carry on seeing this Darren chap, Emily," said William, "We'd like to meet him… invite him over to lunch on Sunday perhaps. And when you go out he can pick you up here from the house. No more of this skulking around…."

Maria was busying herself in one of the kitchen cupboards, unable to face the reality of the conversation she was overhearing. A *man*. A man *fifteen years older* than her daughter.

Emily felt triumphant yet sheepish at the same time. A hollow victory. "OK, dad," she said, "I'll ask him over next weekend."

William nodded, almost too choked to respond. His little girl was going to get hurt and there wasn't a bloody single thing he could do about it.

Emily left the house for Whitemoor Farm and Rascal and William gathered up some paperwork and drove off to work. Maria continued to stare unseeing into the same kitchen cupboard, instinctively knowing that the whole sorry situation would end in tears.

Chapter 20

MARIA PASSED AROUND THE GRAVY BOAT and Darren helped himself to another spoonful of garden peas. The clock on the sideboard ticked loudly, reminding them all that seconds were passing and no one was talking. It was an awkward silence, not a comfortable one and William, aware of his social responsibilities, cast around for something to say.

"How do you find the Sierra, Darren" he asked, "Nice looking motor...."

Maria threw her husband a grateful look and Emily chipped in with comments about the Ford Sierra's higher then average interior specification.

After lunch was over Emily offered to take Darren down to Whitemoor Farm to see Rascal. As the front door shut Maria sank down onto the settee feeling far too drained to consider tackling the dirty dishes and left over food.

"What the hell does she see in him?" she demanded of William.

"I don't know if he's quite that bad, love," said William flopping down beside her.

"Oh Christ, William," she snapped, "Don't start being the bloody diplomat now! He's so much older than her. Oh, it's not just that, of course. I mean, he could be older than her and absolutely wonderful…

it's just that there's something about him I can't put my finger on yet. I don't trust him, William. And those *eyes*...."

"Well, yes," William admitted, "I do know what you mean. Of course I'm not happy about it. Still, it's like I said… there's nothing we can do about it and she's got to learn from her own mistakes. I want to wrap her up in cotton wool and protect her as much as you do but we just can't. Anyway, look on the bright side, love – it'll never last!"

How William was to rue the day he said those words; easy words said with such conviction but with not an ounce of truth in them, for the relationship was to last longer than either of them would have dared imagine.

By the time the new school term was underway and the half term break was looming, Emily had lost all interest in 'A' Levels and university or even going to school at all come to that. All the excitement and freedom which London had promised was surely here already, right here at her fingertips. She felt that by going out with Darren – a real adult who lived in the real adult world – she had leapfrogged the need for exams and any kind of further education. It just seemed juvenile and unnecessary. In her new adult world they sat in Darren's front room smoking dope and drinking whiskey and ginger ale. In her new grown up world she did just enough school work to get by although she had already reached the point of not caring whether she passed or failed any of the 'A' Level subjects she'd taken on with such enthusiasm. What a merciful escape Darren was from her pointless, childish life and how flattering it was that he had chosen her for his attentions. All that rubbish too about him being a 'red-blooded male' and only wanting to 'get into her knickers'. Emily cringed at the memory of her mother's words. She and Darren had been on several dates, or just hung around at his house anyway, before he'd made a move beyond kissing. Emily remembered the night with glee and satisfaction, not for the fact that it had been such a wonderful love-making experience and the earth had moved but for the fact that she had officially 'done it' and was no longer trapped in the body of a naive virgin.

It was just a week before the mock 'A' Level exams in December that Darren produced a plastic bag from his kitchen draw and explained to Emily that the shrivelled up pieces of brown earthy-looking bits were called magic mushrooms.

"What do they do? How do you take them?" she asked, eager and perfectly at ease to take anything that offered a buzz or a temporary high. "How do they make you feel?"

"Well," said Darren, relishing his role of mentor and master in all matters concerning sex, alcohol and illegal drugs, "You eat them in a sandwich, that's the most palatable way in my experience. They usually take a while to kick in – half and hour or so maybe…. Then they make you giggle, really laugh and giggle."

"Yeah? Just like having fun then?"

"Oh yeah, they're only a bit of fun, honestly. You just don't want to stop laughing for ages… everything you see or hear just becomes really funny. Then eventually all the laughing gives way to a really nice floaty feeling. It's not like taking acid – magic mushrooms are really mild. We could have a lot of fun with them tonight, just you and me. I'll put some David Bowie on shall I?"

He went into the lounge and slid 'Tonight' into the mouth of his new CD player. He called back over his shoulder, "Just say if you don't fancy taking them… if you don't feel you're ready…"

Emily rose to the bait liker a fish unable to resist a maggot on a hook.

"Hey, I'll try anything once! Fancy another drink?"

An hour and a half later she was sprawled out on Darren's settee laughing until her ribs ached with the effort of it all. Why had life never seemed so funny before, so utterly amusing and completely hilarious? School wasn't *life*… tidying your bedroom wasn't *life*. Twentieth Century political history and the principles of plate tectonics wasn't *living*. This was living. Having sex, taking drugs, drinking whiskey, strutting about at radio station parties, taking risks, living on the edge. Wasn't this what life was really all about?

By the time Emily had finished the last of her mock exams she was even more convinced that she was merely treading water waiting for the academic year to end. She guessed she'd barely scraped through any of the subjects and the official results only confirmed what she already knew. She hid the truth from Maria and William and gave her teachers false assurances that she would apply herself to her work from now until the real 'A' Level exams the following summer.

For his part Darren poured an endless supply of drinks and rolled an endless supply of joints and assured her that he would be able to put her in the frame for a job at Rocket Sound when she had finished school. What kind of job he never said and Emily didn't ask. For God's sake, people would kill for a job at a radio station so it really didn't matter whether the job turned out to be in sales, promotions, commercial production, news or the record library. Who cared? A *job*, with a *wage*, at a *radio station*… this was the chance of a lifetime and Darren O'Dowel was the person to open that magical door and invite her through.

Darren O'Dowel sat back and watched and bided his time. He was happy to have Emily become increasingly dependent on him. Here was an attractive and bright young woman who could be moulded and manipulated to slot into his lifestyle, a companion to imprint himself upon, a partner who could be shaped and modelled to be the perfect… wife? Yes, that's what he wanted, he decided… a wife who would defer to him, whose thoughts and principles would reflect his own – an obedient, subservient wife who would be grateful to have him as a husband and honoured to be the mother of his children. Mmm, he'd have to play this one very carefully if he was to keep a hold of Emily West. She was so bubbly and bright although that independent, defiant streak may be a difficult trait to break down. Still, give it time… for now he was happy to bask in the glory of having attracted a girl fifteen years his junior and accept the half-envious, good natured jibes of 'cradle snatcher' from his station colleagues.

When Emily eventually began to recognise the subtle methods of control Darren exerted over her she also identified a feeling of being trapped. But the feeling floated in the distance and she could never fully focus on it or understand it completely. It was easier to do as

Darren asked in most cases, seeing as he was so obviously older, wiser and more knowledgeable in life than she was. And in any case the advantages outweighed the disadvantages. She imagined ending her relationship with Darren and in so doing she saw her life collapse into a black hole. What job would she do? She had no ideas and no passions to guide her. How could she go back to being a little girl, reading horse care manuals and helping Maria make jam and biscuits, when she had a taste for whiskey and a mind for adventure? How could she salvage her 'A' Level exams when she could never hope to make up the work that would ensure her some decent grades?

"I think I love you, Emily." Darren said the words quite matter-of-factly one Saturday night when they were lying in his bed together.

"I love you too," she replied, genuinely not knowing whether she meant it or not but feeling it was the only response to give.

"And I trust you completely... and you trust me don't you?"

"Yes... of course I do."

"It's just that there are some things I could share with you, if we're really serious about being together..."

Emily knew he was playing a game with her, enticing her into something as yet unexplained, but her curiosity was on full alert whilst her powers of reasoning were being dulled by drink.

"What kind of things," she demanded, "Come *on* Darren, what?!"

Darren finished rolling a particularly heavy joint and took a long drag from it before answering. "Well, I rather enjoy looking at pornography."

He said this with all the superiority and conviction that someone might have expressing an interest in early aircraft or European history. Emily didn't know what he meant, specifically, or what her reaction was meant to be but didn't want to spoil the night by giving the wrong response.

So she opted for a non-committal and what she hoped was a mature prompt, "And?"

"And... I've got some stuff we can look at together... magazines... videos... fancy it?"

Emily nodded dumbly and waited on the bed whilst Darren sauntered over to the chest of drawers in the corner of the room. He selected a handful of magazines and brought them over to Emily.

"Have you ever seen anything like this before?" he asked, flicking through the pages. "These ones you can just buy from the newsagents... this one here though is hard core from Germany. Oh, and this one's from Sweden."

Emily turned the pages with a combination of anticipation and loathing. The girls in the softer magazines offered up their creamy white bodies in a steady stream of titillating yet structured poses whilst in the foreign publications the models came in all shapes and sizes and looked so engrossed in various sexual acts that they may not have been aware of being photographed at all. Over the last whiskey and ginger ale of the night Darren said, "Go into a newsagent tomorrow and buy Escort and Fiesta from the top shelf."

The command took Emily by surprise. "Hah, no way!"

"Sorry, I forgot you're only a baby... real women don't think twice about taking stuff off the top shelf. In fact, they do it all the time... *real* women..."

Emily smarted at the implication. "Well, why can't you buy them if you want them?" she ventured, nervously.

"Because it's a challenge for you... a test to see if you're really a woman and not just a silly schoolgirl. Of course if you haven't got the balls...."

"Hey! I can do anything... I've told you already, I've got the confidence to do *anything*."

"We'll see, shall we?" said Darren smiling, staring at her with his beady black eyes. "We'll see."

By the spring Maria, William and Emily had reached an uneasy truce over the subject of Darren O'Dowel. When he came to the house he was polite enough and could even be quite charming at times but as soon as he left Maria and William had the same old conversation which centred on the same old theme, 'What on *earth* does she see in him?'

The End of Emily West

In April, anticipating some dire 'A' Level results Emily thought it would be prudent to tell Maria of her immediate vision for the future. Maria was in the kitchen, taking some wet clothes out of the washer.

"I'll give you a hand with those things, mum," offered Emily.

Maria was taken aback at the suggestion, so used was she now to her daughter's mood swings, back chatting and general indifference.

"OK love, thanks. I think it can all go outside on the line for an hour or so."

They made their way to the washing line at the bottom of the garden. Maria pointed out various plants that she hoped would do well this year. Emily politely followed the direction of Maria's finger but could not identify the plants she talked of. Emily was pegging out her third item of damp whites when she finally blurted out, "I don't think I want to go to University, mum."

"Oh, really?" Maria could have danced around the garden with joy, for this meant that her little girl wouldn't be leaving after all. "Well, it's totally up to you of course… your dad and I will support whatever decision you make, you know?"

"Yeah… thanks…"

They finished hanging out the washing and Maria bent down to pick up the empty laundry basket from the grass.

"So… 'A' Levels and then…? Well, you can have a bit of a break, can't you? Any ideas yet what you want to do?"

"Well, Darren says he can probably get me something at Rocket Sound."

In the distance they both heard the 'phone ringing in the house.

"I'll get it!" said Emily and darted back across the lawn.

The snowy white garments skipped and danced in the breeze as Maria turned her back on them and followed her daughter's path up to the house. Just a couple of minutes ago she had felt like dancing but reality had just shot through her and left nothing but a dull ache in her heart. Emily wasn't leaving for university… she was staying, but staying for what? *Bloody Darren O'Dowel* that's what. Maria could bet her life on the fact that no good would come of this liaison. She didn't like him, she didn't trust him and now here he was making vague promises to Emily about future work at the radio station. As Maria entered the kitchen she could tell from the way Emily was talking that it was him on the telephone. She put the kettle on to make a cup of coffee, wondering why being a mother had to be quite so painful.

Her precious daughter and Darren O'Dowel… All she could do was stand by until she was needed to pick up the pieces.

Chapter 21

EMILY WAS SO HUNG OVER FOR her Pure Maths paper that she gave up half way through and closed her eyes. Darren had lent her his company car to drive herself into school but her head was too dull and clouded to appreciate the novelty and showmanship of driving through the school gates and parking up outside the classroom. By the time the whole sorry episode of exam sitting was over Emily knew beyond a shadow of a doubt that she had failed – in fact she hadn't even turned up for one of her geology papers so she knew that was a no hoper. On the day of the last exam when she walked out of the school's front entrance for the final time she made a silent vow never to return. No re-sits and no coming back on the official results day in August. No way. Her school days were over and the door on that time was closed forever. All she had to do now was get on with the rest of her life.

During the time running up to the posting of the results in the school foyer, she dropped enough hints to Maria and William to seriously lessen their expectations. Feeling somewhat guilty but in the spirit of personal survival she maintained the pretence that she had worked really hard but the exam questions didn't go her way on the day. Quite how much her parents were deceived by this she never knew but she was grateful for the fact that they didn't make an issue of it.

The summer holidays started and the day of the results loomed ahead. Emily spent virtually all her time either with Rascal at Whitemoor Farm or at Darren's house. Maria and William appeared to accept the fact that she stayed over there about four nights out of seven and they all jogged along with the arrangement in an uncomfortable, embarrassed silence. Darren still maintained that he could get her a foot in the door at Rocket Sound 'when the time was right' and Emily held on to her relationship with him never knowing if she was happy or sad, satisfied or frustrated. Did she love him? She didn't know, or was she mistaking love for the dependence on him she felt so absorbed by. The relationship itself wasn't particularly loving but as Darren consistently pointed out, she had a lot to learn. He was quick to tell her where she was going wrong – everything from matters of speech and grammar to how she could make more of her physical attributes. The fact was however, that the utterly directionless Emily was happy, or at least resigned, to go along with this in order to embrace the new grown up life which Darren O'Dowel represented. The other fact was that Emily had such a narrow field of vision when it came to Darren's attitude and behaviour she would have been genuinely surprised if she had been told that any female worth her salt would not have put up with him.

Exactly when she had gone from a bright and confident girl to one who appeared to be constantly treading on egg shells she could never quite pinpoint, but she did accept that life with Darren was not all easy. She had to second guess his mood in order to have a peaceful time with him. She had to be careful what she said in case she came across as thick or naive and it was best not to contradict him or go against his wishes if she didn't want to face his fierce sulks or flashes of anger. She feared him yet craved his love and devotion. She stubbornly ignored his faults because she was blinded by the notion of a happy ever after ending. She wanted him to be something he was not and despite the many facts staring her in the face she strove to believe that one day he would change and turn into the loving partner her dreams were made of.

The night before the 'A' Levels results were out, Emily was lying with Darren in his bed, drinking and smoking and flicking though the soft porn magazines that she felt regularly pressured into taking down

The End of Emily West

from the top shelf and purchasing. Darren drank them in greedily but there was an edge to his manner tonight which she knew meant trouble.

"Just look at these girls," he said, forcefully, without subtlety. "You could look like these girls… if you tried."

Emily bristled at the inference that she was in some way not measuring up to the plastic models in their impossible poses.

"What do you mean? How?"

"Well, you could dress up more for me in the bedroom… look at what she's wearing for instance… wouldn't you like to wear something like that?"

Emily studied the Barbie blonde with her bronzed skin and enormous breasts. She was wearing an electric blue sequined bra, a matching tutu and acid yellow stiletto heels. She was standing with her legs set provocatively apart and with her forefinger up to her mouth she displayed a look of wide-eyed surprise. Her body, with its long silky limbs and flawless skin was bordering on perfection and Emily felt suddenly lumpy and inadequate in comparison.

She felt hurt and betrayed but managed the doubtful response, "I suppose… I've never though about it before…"

"Mmm…" pondered Darren. "You're shorter and heavier set, of course… maybe if you lost a bit of that puppy fat…."

Emily crashed and stumbled her way through the rest of the night, mortified that she should be thought of by Darren as in any way overweight. When she had last stood on the bathroom scales she was a pound short of eight stone. Surely that was reasonable? But Darren had knocked her confidence and she withdrew into a shell which made him more annoyed and her increasingly resistant. The following morning he went silently to work and she made her way back home.

He'll ring, she thought. *I know he'll ring this morning because he knows the 'A' Level results are out today.* But he didn't call. At lunchtime Jackie Dean 'phoned to say that she had been into school to collect her results. She'd got a C in English Literature and a B in general studies.

"Hey, well done, Jackie!" said Emily. "I suppose you checked mine? I didn't get any did I?" She laughed, full of bravado but her voice threatened to crack under the strain of the day. Why hadn't Darren called her? Was he really punishing her for last night and her resistance to dress up like a showgirl? What if he didn't call her to ask her to his house tonight? By the time this evening came she would want to murder a glass or two of whiskey and be glad to lose herself in a warm fuzzy haze of dope. She ended the conversation with Jackie and trudged into the kitchen.

"Never mind, love," said Maria who by now was under no illusions about today's results. "There's more to life than exam results, isn't there?" Then, suspecting that Darren hadn't called, "Shall you be going over to Darren's tonight?"

"Er, I'm not sure mum, actually… I think I'll just go up and have a bath…."

Maria let her go upstairs before breathing out a huge sigh and muttering out "Damn him," under her breath. How could her beautiful, intelligent daughter put up with such a self-centred, inconsiderate idiot as Darren O'Dowel?! How long would it be before she saw him for what he was? And how long would Maria have to be on standby, waiting for the day when the scales would drop from her daughter's eyes? *Any day now* she prayed, *any day now*. She waited until she heard the bath water running upstairs before asking directory enquiries to give her the number for Rocket Sound. Having got through to Darren in the engineering department she forced herself to be as friendly as possible and asked Darren if he could please call Emily as she had received some rather disappointing news about her 'A' Level results. Sounding equally as friendly Darren assured her that he would call her that afternoon. When eventually he did the change in Emily was like a light suddenly flooding a darkened room. She put on make-up and perfume and sauntered out of the door and Maria almost tasted bile in her throat such was the sick feeling of utter helplessness.

When William arrived home that night he wrote Emily a note of sympathy and support about her results and left it on her dressing table. He was gutted by it but knew that accusations and recriminations would be of little use now. And in any case he felt acutely as ever that he and Maria were living on a knife edge with their daughter. He suspected that she enjoyed a drink or two too many with Darren O'Dowel and he'd been mortified to find an empty packet of cigarettes in the car's glove box. What kind of path was this man leading her down? And wasn't it time he or Maria tackled the matter head on? He sat down on Emily's bed and mulled over the answer which he now knew off by heart. *If they tackled her and she rebelled they may lose her forever and they loved her too much to take that chance.*

It was some time before William found the strength in his legs to get up off the bed and walk downstairs.

Chapter 22

From that September Emily began to go in to Rocket Sound for three or four mornings a week. She lent a hand to whichever department needed her the most – a job without pay which was actually excessive coffee fetching heavily disguised as work experience. However, Maria and William recognised that she seemed happy with this, describing it more as a 'year off' until a firm job offer came along from Rocket or she decided upon something else. They had no idea of the bombshell that was about to be dropped on their lives.

It was the first Saturday in October and Emily said that Darren would like to come round for dinner. For Emily's sake Maria in particular embraced the idea and went to great efforts with home made desserts, crystal cut glasses and her best embroidered table cloth and napkins. All in all the meal and all the social niceties which surrounded it went well. Emily was particularly bright-eyed and chatty and William did his usual sterling job of keeping the conversation going when it may have flagged. After dessert Maria brought them all coffee and it was then that Darren made a big show of clearing his throat and announcing that he had something to ask William. Emily's eyes darted from Maria to William and she let out a barely audible squeal of excitement. Maria felt her throat constrict and almost shrivel with dryness. She placed her half raised cup down on its saucer again for fear of dropping it. Time itself seemed to stand still as she waited for the question which she knew was coming.

"Mr West," said Darren, "I'd like to ask you for your daughter's hand in marriage."

He has nothing to offer my daughter, thought Maria looking into the blackness of his eyes. *He is shallow. He is calculating. He has no soul.*

Darren had asked the question with all the pomp and confidence of someone who is not used to being refused and with all the smugness of someone who knows they could have gone ahead with their plans whether they were agreed to or not.

William was the first to speak.

"Well! Er, yes, well… you have taken us by surprise, haven't they, Maria?" He looked at Emily willing her or Darren to confess that this was all just a big silly joke. But they didn't. They both just sat there smiling and waiting, expecting a response.

"Well, if that's what you both want… if you think you're going to be happy…"

Emily had no doubt at all that she was going to be happy for it was a certainty that Darren would change when they were married. He'd told her all about his past, about his first wife who he had truly loved but who had taken a drugs overdose when she found out she couldn't have children, about his remote and cold parents and his now compelling need to have someone to love and rely on. He told her he wanted to have someone he could treat like a princess, a goddess even – a precious vessel who would carry his children. He wanted someone who understood him completely, someone who wouldn't defy him or undermine him… someone who would trust him implicitly and follow his lead, no matter what. Yes, Darren might be difficult now, hurtful and dismissive sometimes, commanding and domineering even at others, but then who wouldn't be with that kind of past? What he obviously needed was a stable home life and a loving wife and it was down to her, Emily, to provide both.

"We've lost her… that's it! He's taken her from us!" Maria was rocking back and forth on the settee whilst William paced up and down. Then Maria considered another new and terrifying thought.

"What if they move? What if his job takes him hundreds of miles away from here?!"

William paused and threw up his hands, knowing that his words would offer little comfort.

"Then so be it, I'm afraid… she's officially an adult and this is apparently what she wants. I don't like it any more than you do – she's too young and he's too old and quite apart from that we don't actually *like* the man. But it's her life. We can't wrap her up in cotton wool and we can't keep her here forever."

"If only Bobby was alive… if only we still had Bobby…"

William sat down beside her and held her close. "I know, love, I know…"

"At least he could tell his big sister she's being a silly little fool!" Maria sobbed.

"And she'd insist on him being a page boy just to get him back for that!"

Maria closed her eyes and hated the vision that crept out of the blackness. A bride and groom at the altar with a trail of bridesmaids behind them… and an empty space where Bobby should be. Maria pulled herself up for having a vision of Bobby as a small child. Of *course* he wouldn't be a little page boy following the bridesmaids… he'd be an usher, tall and lanky, shy and awkward as he handed out the order of service and directed people to their seats in the church. The vision blurred and faded for however long she lived, however many years went by, Bobby would not age. Bobby would forever be her baby boy.

Chapter 23

THE FIRST TIME THAT EMILY WITNESSED Darren's violent temper was on April 1st, just a few weeks before they were due to be married. How appropriate that date, Emily thought much later. How fitting to be able to look back and realise what a fool she'd been taken for on April 1st.

Since their engagement the previous October Emily had moved in with Darren. It was a perfectly decent house although not in the same league as Oakside Grange and in one heated argument Darren had accused Emily of 'slumming it' at his house before running back home to the comforts provided by mummy and daddy. Emily promptly moved in to demonstrate her commitment. She never thought how this clumsily executed move would have been so much better if handled with some tact and sensitivity. All she cared about was stuffing clothes and shoes and books into all manner of bags and boxes and getting over to Darren's house as soon as possible in order to keep him happy. At Christmas that year Darren provided Emily with the only thing she was ever truly thankful to him for – a chocolate Labrador puppy she called Cocoa. The adorable bundle of soft brown fur just about made up for the fact that the rest of her Christmas presents from Darren consisted of an upright vacuum cleaner, a food mixer and a new kettle. Darren came out with the cliché, a wife should be a maid in the kitchen and a whore in the bedroom and against a backdrop of Christmas cheer Emily forced herself to believe that he was only joking.

From the beginning of the New Year Maria and William, as the bride's parents, set to work to give their daughter the wedding she wanted. The church was booked, a cake was ordered, invites were sent out, a white satin dress was fitted and paid for and a deposit was sent to The Unicorn Hotel for the reception. Darren had balked at the prices he'd been quoted for honeymoon packages and eventually, with some six weeks to go, he booked a fly-drive package to the Greek island of Crete, the reasoning being that they were less likely to be ripped off if they could choose their hotels once they were there.

It was on April 1st that Emily mentioned to Darren that she and Maria had visited not only the dressmakers that afternoon but also the local job centre. He looked up sharply from his dinner and stared at her as he chewed on a mouthful of chicken breast.

When he eventually swallowed it he asked, "What for?"

Emily could read his moods well by now and knew instantly that he was not pleased. Her mind raced, thinking of a way to retract the words but they were still floating in the air between them, stretching and distorting until Darren said, "I'll ask again, shall I? What did you go to the job centre for?"

With a sharp snap Emily suddenly realised that she had nothing to hide and her reasons for visiting the job centre had been totally reasonable.

"Well, mum suggested it may be a good idea to keep my options open… I mean, no firm offer of paid work has come from Rocket yet and although you know I love it there it would be nice to have my own money and have a job that keeps me busy all day… what do you think?"

"I think," said Darren slowly, "I think that you need to pour me another drink."

Emily dutifully poured him another whiskey and ginger ale and tried to keep her mood light-hearted and relaxed as Darren finished his

The End of Emily West

meal and drink in silence. He reached over to the whiskey bottle and filled up his glass again, draining half of its contents in one easy go.

"So… what else do I think?" Darren was menacing now, dark eyed and ready to pounce.

"I don't know… stop it Darren… what's wrong? What have I done wrong?"

"Wrong?!" Darren left his chair to lurch over to Emily. He grabbed her viciously by the arm and dragged her off her chair and onto the floor. She'd been taken off guard and let out a cry of anguish as she felt her cheek rub painfully against the course grain of the carpet.

"I'll tell you what's fucking *wrong*! You and your interfering bitch of a mother don't give two shits about what I've done for you. I got you in the door at Rocket – Christ, they wouldn't have looked at a little tart like you twice if it wasn't for me. And you're so stuck up you want to throw it all back in my face!"

Emily sat up but didn't know what to do. She cowered and covered her face with her hands as Darren picked up his dinner plate and smashed it down onto the table, breaking it into pieces.

"Darren, *please…*"

"And you haven't stopped to think have you - 'cos you're so fucking selfish – you haven't even thought that if you get a full time job away from me you won't be able to be here when I get home from work, when I *need* you. Tea on the table when I get in from work – it's not too much to fucking well ask, is it? You're going to be my *wife* aren't you? You're going to be able to do what wives *do* aren't you?"

Emily heard a voice inside her head whisper, *you don't deserve this. Surely you don't deserve this?* Then the voice screamed the words so loudly that she let them well up inside her and erupt with all the heat and ferocity of a volcano. "What have I done to deserve this? You're trying to control what I do, Darren! You make marrying you sound like a fucking prison sentence! That was it sounds like, fucking prison! I've got a life as well you know!"

Whatever else Emily was about to shout was drowned out by Darren's scream as he pulled her to her feet by her hair. She jerked away from him and he was left with clumps of her blonde locks matted through his fingers. She reached the front door in the hallway before he caught up with her and pinned her up against it.

"You go," Darren said, assaulting her senses with the stink of whiskey and the threat of an attack, "You go and leave this house now and I'll take a knife to the dog."

Emily's eyes reached over to Cocoa's who was sitting on his tail half way up the stairs.

Darren rammed her up against the hardwood of the door, shouting and spitting in her face, "Shall I do it now? Shall I take a knife to the fucking dog right now?"

Emily cried as her natural defence system collapsed, for at that moment she knew that Darren meant what he said. There was to be no arguing now, no fighting, no leaving, no more challenges. Darren had found a sure fire way to hurt her and he knew it. In a second he was pounding up the stairs towards the dog.

Emily screamed out, a strangled, "No!"

Cocoa whined and whimpered as Darren picked him up by the collar and scrambled back down the stairs to Emily. He held him high off the ground until the wide-eyed Cocoa coughed and spluttered, his own collar threatening to choke him.

"This is what I'd like to do to *you*," he spat, thrusting the petrified Cocoa towards Emily before running up the stairs to the bedroom and banging the door shut behind him.

Emily took Cocoa into the living room and shakily made herself a drink. She stroked and whispered to Cocoa whilst pouring drink after drink, eventually forgoing the ginger ale altogether in an attempt to let the whiskey ease her pain more quickly. She felt numb and shell-shocked and frightened as she heard Darren move about in the room above. She'd never seen anyone act like that before. She didn't know *anyone* who had a temper like the one she'd just seen. Something must be terribly wrong to make him do and say those things. He must be worried about something and like a blundering fool she had ridden rough-shod over it, never realising what a dreadful reaction she'd provoke, never imagining that he would lash out so cruelly at the person he loved so much.

The End of Emily West

As the hours passed and the house descended into darkness she began to justify his behaviour, or at the very least pass it off as a totally one-off, out-of-character outburst. Why would he be marrying her if he really felt so violently towards her? And surely he wanted her at Rocket Sound and to be here when he got home only because he truly loved and wanted her? Only a tiny part of Emily ever raised the question, *what if I called off the wedding?* In truth she never, ever, fully considered it as an option. People didn't cancel perfectly planned, expensive, imminent weddings just because of a stupid fight which had all been based on love and fear and misunderstanding, did they? Emily didn't consider the option because she didn't want to face the consequences… the climb-down, the admission of mistakes, the humiliation, the I-told-you-sos… so when Darren came into the living room at four o'clock in the morning and got down on his knees and begged her for forgiveness, she was only too happy to take him in her arms and do as he asked.

Chapter 24

THE DAY OF THE WEDDING WAS clear and mild for May and the last minute preparations that morning took place at Oakside Grange in a flurry of nervous energy. Maria lurched from one emotion to the next; desperately wanting to tell Emily it wasn't too late to call the whole thing off yet not wanting to spoil what should be such a special day. She fussed around with the hem of Jackie Dean's bridesmaid's dress and checked that the two little ones, Emily's young cousins, had been to the toilet and blown their noses. She mentally thanked no one in particular that there was so much to do she actually didn't have the time to think too deeply about the implications of the forthcoming ceremony. Still, she reasoned, there was a lot to be thankful for... Emily and Darren were not moving away and she and her daughter still had a relationship of sorts. It was just that... well, she hated to see Emily fawn over Darren so much, deferring to him and almost having to ask his permission over even the most trivial of things. She could be loving one minute and snappy the next and Maria wondered what had happened to her happy-go-lucky little girl. She went upstairs and checked the spare room. Bizarrely, today was the first time she and William would be meeting Darren's parents, Albert and Elsa, and they were staying at Oakside for the night. Albert's teaching work had taken them to France for two years so they had only spoken on the 'phone. They sounded alright but Maria was curious to meet the people who between them had spawned the creature who had taken over her daughter's life so comprehensively.

Back downstairs in the hallway the wedding party was waiting for the cars to arrive that would take them to St Matthew's church. Maria forced herself to believe what a happy day this was; a wedding day, a spectacular show of love and commitment. She had to think this for fear of slipping into those dark suppressed thoughts of that other event at St Matthew's – that heartbreaking day when they had said goodbye to Bobby and laid him to rest.

When they got to the church, Maria took her place at the front and continued to play out her role as mother-of-the-bride to perfection. She nodded and smiled at family and friends and greeted Albert and Elsa with outstretched arms and as much good grace as she could muster. Darren stood in his appointed place, smug in the knowledge this whole snooty, middleclass congregation was about to witness his marriage to a teenage bride and in spite of what he was sure they were all thinking there wasn't a damn thing any of them could do about it.

Outside in the church porch, William linked his arm through Emily's.

"Couple of minutes to go love, I think," he said. "Are you all set? Old, new, borrowed and blue and all that?"

"Yes, Dad – Mum thought of pretty much everything…"

"I've got something old in my pocket," said William suddenly. "Want to see it?" And before Emily could even give a reply he was fishing his wallet out of his suit jacket pocket. Leafing through some notes and receipts he came to what he was looking for.

"Look! Bet you didn't know I've carried that around with me for all these years."

Emily looked at the photograph. It was worn at the edges and there was a slight crease cutting across the top left hand corner. But even these imperfections couldn't diminish the picture itself, couldn't take away the obvious happiness of the moment it was taken or the simple innocent pride it exuded.

"No," whispered Emily, "No, dad I didn't…"

Wendy Turner Webster

"Your first day at school… your mum and I were so proud of you, Emily… and we still are you know."

"Dad…"

"Hey, I can hear music!" And William hastily put the photograph and the wallet back into his pocket as they heard the organ player hit the first few notes of Wagner's Bridal Chorus.

Taking her last few steps as a single woman Emily made a determined effort not to think about her absent usher, blocking all thoughts of him out of her mind completely. She did, however, think about two other people who could not be here with her today… She had wanted Karen Black to be a bridesmaid as well as Jackie, in spite of not having seen her for a few years and only keeping in touch on an erratic basis. But a telephone conversation with Jackie's mum revealed that Jackie had joined the army some six months previously and in no way could get leave for the date of the wedding. Emily had replaced the telephone receiver in shocked disbelief. The *army*. How life had moved on for both of them, taking twists and turns which neither of them could ever have predicted, these two inseparable beings who were going to go to college together, share a flat together and take on the world. Still staring at the mute telephone Emily had wondered whether Karen still thought of The Jam, as she often did, and secretly wondered what life would be like now if Paul, Bruce and Rick had scooped them up and whisked them away, as they were meant to have done. The other person she thought of was Paul Andrew. They had kept in touch by letter when he first went off to his new life in Australia, but it soon became obvious to Emily that he had really settled there and would not be coming home as promised. They hadn't written to each other for almost two years when Emily put pen to paper and told Paul of her impending wedding to Darren. It was a forced, stilted kind of letter and he had written back immediately with formal messages of congratulations and good luck for the future. Another friend who was already a distant memory.

Time and tide wait for no man.

And as the Bridal Chorus came to an end Emily took her place alongside Darren, smiling up at him, ready to be his wife.

Chapter 25

"**Phew!**" **Maria breathed a sigh of** relief as she closed the front door and turned back to William, "Thank God that's over. What did you make of them?"

It was Sunday afternoon and Albert and Elsa had just left Oakside Grange.

"Well, I felt quite sorry for her."

"Oh, so did I… she could hardly speak without him sticking his oar in! She looked completely defeated most of the time. And he was so *pompous*. Didn't you get the feeling he was trying to be smarter than us… kept saying little things which made him out to be intellectually superior?"

"Yes," agreed William, "I know exactly what you mean – the bloody cheek of it!"

"Not too difficult to see where Darren gets his attitude from, is it? God, I felt like reaching for the dictionary to make sense of some of those words Albert was dropping into the conversation! But it was all just a big show – big words to try and make a big impression."

"Come on, love. Let's take Cocoa for a walk down to Whitemoor Farm and see to Rascal – I could do with some air…"

Emily woke up on Sunday afternoon at one o'clock. She woke up but her head felt thick and heavy so she kept her eyes shut against the light of the outside world. She could feel the warmth of Darren's body in the hotel bed beside her. Another night in this local hotel and then a flight tomorrow to Crete. *Then the magic would begin* she promised herself. What more could a newly married couple need to ignite their passion than the backdrop of a sun-kissed Greek island? Through the muggy haze of last night's excessive quantities of whiskey and dope Emily mulled over the wedding. It really had been a perfect day and she was proud of the gold band that Darren had placed so lovingly on her finger. She had been the focus of everyone's attention and a steady stream of guests had made a point of telling her how beautiful she looked and how lucky Darren was to have such a wonderful bride on his arm. The guests had mostly been on her side of the family. Apart from his parents and a few colleagues from Rocket Sound Darren hadn't felt inclined to invite any of his blood relations, claiming that he hardly had any. Emily thought it was sad and really hoped that Darren would embrace her family and make it his own. But already this notion seemed too optimistic and Darren had even spoiled some of her memory of the day with his reluctance to give her side of the family a fighting chance…. She'd seen him give a withering glance to his father when William had praised Maria for all her hard work and she'd been acutely embarrassed because other people must have seen it too. He'd made a stage-whispered cruel jibe about the dress her Aunty Bea was wearing – lovely old Aunty Bea who was famed within the family for her one-off designs and unique fashion sense. And that hurtful, sneering comment when they'd driven off in his car, cans and old shoes clattering behind them on pieces of string and shaving cream hearts obscuring the view from the windows; *"Thank fuck we're escaping from that rabble of half brains."* Emily had laughed off the comment for fear of challenging it and sparking a row, but why were they half-brains? Why did Darren think so little of them when he hardly *knew* any of her extended family? For herself she was trying really hard to live up to Darren's expectations of her; *a maid in the kitchen and a whore in the bedroom,* whilst at the same time trying to keep up with world news, new book publications and local politics. Darren could so easily put anyone down as being 'thick' and 'lacking in education'. He positively seemed to despise people who were content with their lives and it was a constant battle for Emily to stay in his esteemed favour.

After about half an hour had passed Darren stirred beside her. He stretched and yawned and hooked one of her legs in his, pulling them apart. Emily's eyes were still shut as his fingers worked their way roughly inside her.

"My beautiful, dutiful wife," he said laughing at his play on words. He pulled his fingers out and jammed them into her mouth. "Lick," he commanded, "Lick yourself off my fingers…. Now go and put on your wedding dress."

Emily gasped as the force of the plane taking off compelled her to sit firmly back in her seat. She'd never been in an aeroplane before and had been really looking forward to this part of their honeymoon adventure. Darren laughed at her child-like excitement and Emily settled back to enjoy the journey and read through, once again, all the material she had gathered on Crete. She was glad they had taken off at last; their charter flight had been delayed in taking off for some three hours which had made Darren tense and irritable. Still, now they were finally on their way and surely Darren was ready to relax and embrace this week of sunshine and romance as much as she was? They bought some wine from the drinks trolley and when Darren put on a pair of headphones to listen to some music, Emily stared out of the window and began to imagine what the week would bring. Her thoughts drifted lazily through a maze of sun-soaked images; baked earth and lush olive groves, beach hotels with cool and elegant marble foyers, spacious rooms with bathrobes and slippers, old crones sitting outside village cafes – sipping thick black coffee and making lace tablecloths. And leather-skinned men herding goats down twisting, dusty lanes – a vision so clear she could almost smell the clumps of sage and thyme growing by the roadside.

How quickly these images were shattered when they landed at Herakleion airport at midnight, sticky and tired and still faced with the task of completing all the paperwork required at the car hire desk and finding a hotel for the night. After arguing about whether to turn this way or that or to stop at this hotel or that hotel a tearful Emily folded up her map as Darren turned the unfamiliar, uncooperative car down a side road on the outskirts of the city and turned off the engine.

"This'll do, for fuck's sake," he said and Emily looked out of her window at the faded sign of The Bluebird Hotel. It had a single star by its name and so naturally did not have the elegant marbled reception complete with luscious flower arrangements and uniformed staff which Emily had been dreaming of for the first night of their honeymoon.

"We'll get somewhere better tomorrow," said Darren dismissively, oblivious to her deep disappointment and he dragged their luggage into the small, dimly lit lobby. A bored looking man sat on a stool behind a rickety old desk, a magazine in one hand and a cigarette in the other. The prospect of a booking didn't seem to bother him one way or the other and after a short conversation with Darren in pidgin English he slid the key for room number eight across the counter, quickly turning back to his magazine and what was left of his cigarette.

In the room Emily hardly dared speak for fear of crying. She opened her case and decided against wearing the pretty cream lace slip she'd bought especially for this night. She padded into the bathroom to brush her teeth. There were hairs in the bath, a dead cockroach lay shrivelled up in the corner of the poky little room and above the tiny wash hand basin the mirror was cracked and mottled with age. Emily looked into the mirror and stared deep into her own eyes. Was this it? Was this crushing disappointment the best that was on offer? Wouldn't it be wonderful if she and Darren could sit on the clapped out iron bed with its moth eaten sheets and giggle about the ridiculousness of the situation… pull together in adversity instead of falling apart under the pressure of it all going wrong. The bed creaked predictably as she climbed into it and pulled the sheets over her naked body. The bed creaked and Darren snored and Emily could only console herself with the thought that tomorrow would be a better day.

It wasn't. Emily dressed herself up to the nines and put on full make-up before realising that the casual nature of a fly-drive holiday and the Mediterranean heat demanded neither of these things. By mid-morning she felt overdressed and self-conscious, and in this car which did not have the luxury of air-conditioning her carefully applied make-up was clogging up in unattractive patches around her face and neck. By mid-morning it appeared they had driven in totally the opposite direction to the one Darren had planned. She blamed him for rushing her when she needed more time to study the map and he blamed her for being a typical female who couldn't tell north from south and east from west.

"Maybe an 'A' Level or two wouldn't have come amiss after all," he snapped.

Emily bristled at his jibe and smacked the map against the dashboard.

"Oh, why don't you navigate then you smart arse?" she screamed. And in the split second of silence that followed she knew she should have bitten through her tongue rather than have said those words.

"You little *bitch!*" Darren spat out the words and a spray of salvia splattered the inside of the windscreen. At the same time his right hand left the steering wheel and the back of it hit Emily full in the mouth. She screamed in terror and surprise and looked down on her lap to see blood dripping onto her dress. She covered her face with her hands and sobbed whilst Darren steered the car with one hand and held the road map in the other.

"What a fucking load of crap this is," he said eventually. "Some shitty honeymoon, eh?"

They drove on in complete silence until two o'clock when they reached the picturesque old harbour in Rethymnon. If there was any magic to be had on the island of Crete, if there had ever been a glimpse of happiness in prospect, any warmth or any love, it was not here now. The brightly painted little sailing boats danced on the water and the sun beat down from a Wedgwood blue sky… it was the scene from a picture postcard yet Emily hardly noticed it as she trailed behind Darren to a waterfront restaurant. Emily hadn't put on any sun cream and her fair skin began to itch and prickle. The sun became a spiteful ball of fire heaping further misery upon her already miserable day and she was grateful at least for the shade provided by the parasol over their table. They ordered white wine and Darren merely shrugged as Emily declined the offer of food. He studied the menu in great detail before ordering pizza and garlic bread for himself.

After the first glass of wine had been drained he leant forward and said, "Why did you have to annoy me? Why did you have to say something that would make me do that to you? I never *had* a temper until I met you, you know? If I get mad it's because you make me!" He paused and then hissed in her ear, "No one calls me a smart arse and gets away with it, understand?"

Emily nodded dumbly and drowned her misery in her wine. If she drank enough maybe this whole day would fade into a warm black hole of blissful sleep. Maybe the whole week would. It was worth a try.

Two hours later Emily came round and found herself being propelled up some steps at the back of the restaurant. Darren was jabbing her in the small of the back with a bottle of whiskey.

"You stupid fucking cow! I've had to pay for those glasses you knocked over. Everyone in the place was staring at you. Well, I'm not doing any more fucking driving now – this room's available for two nights and I intend to get in it and get completely fucking pissed. You can go off and do what the fuck you like."

Emily could only think of returning to the blessed relief of her black hole and as soon as Darren went into the bathroom she unscrewed the cap off the bottle of whiskey and drank several huge mouthfuls. Darren came back into the room as she was about to drink some more but he snatched the bottle from her and pushed her onto the bed.

"Oh, go to fucking sleep," she heard him say. Then the room began to swim and the blackness wrapped itself around her, as welcome as a huge velvet cloak on a bitter winter's night.

When she came to again it was dark outside. In a half conscious haze she found herself spread eagle on the bed. She felt the tension of material pulled tightly around her wrists and wondered how she had come to be tied up like this. Her head felt painfully heavy and her tongue felt thick and dry. As her ears grew attuned to the sounds of the night she heard Darren panting and groaning nearby. She lifted her head up a few inches and through fluttering eyelids could just make out the fact that Darren was kneeling between her legs, facing her, desperately trying to wank himself off onto a thick slice of honeydew melon. The lights from the harbour below cast a warm orange glow over part of the ceiling and she could hear laughter and the chink of glasses from the restaurant under their balcony. She closed her eyes tightly shut and willed herself to slip away. What did she have to do? How desperate did she have to be for her senses to give in and shut down, sending her into that darkened place where the fingers of pain never quite reached?

It wouldn't come. The state of oblivion refused to take a hold and she heard Darren cry out as if in pain when he finally achieved his long awaited orgasm. She felt the tears trickle slowly down each side of her face, burning tears of shame and despair. She tried to say, *Darren please*, but the dry throat and thick tongue conspired against her, refusing to let her speak. She raised her head once more to look at him, her husband, begging him with her eyes. But he wasn't looking at Emily's face. He was busying himself with the semen-soaked slice of melon, muttering and laughing like a mad thing as he pushed it up inside her. When it had all disappeared he held a bottle of wine to her lips. She gulped at it greedily until eventually he withdrew it.

"That's it, baby," he crooned. "That's my obedient little girl. See how good things can be when you do as you're told?" And as Emily drifted in and out of her beloved blackness, so it went on until morning.

Darren was almost jovial by the time they had both sobered up some twenty four hours later. He burst into their room to tell her with some glee that he had managed to book it for a further two nights. Emily heard her own small voice inside her head but it was too weak and tired to be of any use. *I wanted to see the island. I wanted to see the beaches and the olive groves and the beautiful hotels.* But Darren was grabbing for her hands and chattering away in her face. Eventually she picked up the thread of what he was saying.

"... stay here, we may as well. We can eat and drink and fuck all day and night.... So beautiful when you do what you're told... all you have to do is submit to me.... please don't make me angry anymore Emily...."

She felt numb and wretched and decidedly dehydrated as later on they walked hand in hand around the harbour, stopping to look at fish in the water or at some trinket in a local shop. And she was completely confused. Darren was being so nice and normal today it was as if the anger and rage of the last couple of days hadn't really taken place at all. Emily tried to push those hateful images out of her mind but however successful she was in blocking them out she had to admit to herself that this was not what she'd expected married life to be like. When she thought how her mum and dad were with each other, how they pulled together, how they respected each other... well, she had assumed that her marriage would be like that. Perhaps it still could be. Perhaps she had to work harder... perhaps she had to support Darren more, agree with him more and accept that he was right about everything he had an opinion on. After all, she did seem to make him angry, did seem to provoke a level of violence which he claimed he'd never felt before.

When they left Rethymnon there was no point in heading any further west. They were only here for a week and so they joined the main road again, east towards Irakleion, stopping half way at Bali Beach. There were several tavernas on the beachfront and some simple whitewashed guest houses. The guide book described these hotel alternatives as 'rooms-for-rent', or *domatia*. They checked into one of these for the last two nights of their honeymoon and as soon as their bags were installed in their room they took towels, books and sun cream and found a spare patch of sand on the beach. Darren immediately stolled down to the water and started wading in. Emily had never been much of a swimmer and so stayed sitting on her beach towel rubbing in sun cream. Darren waved at her and she waved back. It was at that moment on Bali Beach, sitting there alone, completely isolated from her friends and family, that she felt bound and gagged, suffocated almost by the weight of depression. The beach world around her slipped into slow motion as she sat paralysed on the sand, fearful of the future and scarred by the past, suspended in the present which was the most frightening place of all.

Emily had never known such anxiety before, such nervousness and raw fear and in a moment of startling thought which flashed in front of her like sheet lightening she wondered if Bobby had felt frightened just before he died. The thought made her feel physically sick and she wondered how she could have jogged through the last few years never having asked herself that question. *Because it was easier to block it out, to forget Bobby, to deny how much she missed him.*

Looking out to the vastness of the Mediterranean Sea, the bubble of her past burst, spewing out all its pent up contents in one powerful rush of emotion. She sat and sobbed for her little brother and for all the years she'd tried to wipe out his existence. He deserved better than that, better than a sister with a stone inside her instead of a heart. He deserved to be remembered, to be spoken about, to be missed at her wedding. Her face burned with shame and regret when she remembered how she had gone through the whole wedding at St Matthew's church shutting out Bobby in case he upset her day. He should have been there. He shouldn't be dead. He should have been there.

Dripping with salt water and running his fingers through his sopping wet hair, Darren made his way up the beach and sat down on his towel beside Emily.

"What's the matter?" he asked as Emily wiped her eyes and blew her nose, and for one moment Emily dared to hope that he might be sympathetic, might hold her close to his chest and show some compassion when she told him what she was going through.

"It's Bobby," she began and her voice cracked and faltered as she struggled with the words. "I was thinking… he should have been there on our wedding day…"

Having towelled himself dry Darren began to cover himself with sun cream. "For God's sake! We're here on our honeymoon and you have to come up with morbid thoughts like that! I'm in a good mood today, so give it a rest will you?"

Emily scrambled to her feet and grabbed the key to their room, mumbling that she had to go to the toilet. The truth was that she wanted to run and run and run and never stop; away from Darren, away from this island, away from her pit of despair. She bought a bottle of ouzo and took it back to the room. Darren could be as angry as he liked – all she wanted to do was drink herself asleep. As the clear liquid burnt its way down her throat she dared to wonder whether marrying Darren O'Dowel hadn't been a mistake. It was so painful to ask the question yet so easy to answer it. Yes, it had been a mistake. But how could she go home and admit to it? How could she repeat and relive the scenes of violence and malicious words, the nights of drunkenness, of smoking dope, and admit to having sex that was not fun and loving but simply cruel and degrading? She was living a life she was ashamed of and could think of no easy way out of it. The shame would have to be her own guilty secret. And anyway, how could she possibly let everyone down who had worked so hard to give her such a wonderful white wedding?

She had brought all this upon herself. She had stubbornly made her own bed… and for better or worse, now she must lie in it.

Chapter 26

DARREN FINISHED OFF HIS CONVERSATION WITH Lenny, Rocket Sound's Head of Commercial Production, and left the 'Com Prod' studio clutching three examples of radio commercial scripts and a brief for the creation of a new one. The job of Commercial Script Writer was about to become available and Darren wanted Emily to have it. She was bright and creative and had a decent enough command of the English language so he had no doubt she was up to it. What's more it would fit in with him perfectly; she'd be under his wing all day and every day and keeping exactly the same hours as him.

Mmm… Emily, his Emily… unfortunately she wasn't as compliant and instantly submissive as he would have liked and more often than not it really pissed him off. Sometimes she just made him see red and then she had the fucking face to wonder why he lashed out. Well, Christ! With some women it got to a point and that was the only language they seemed to understand. He did usually regret those episodes… usually… and luckily Emily was always ready to forgive and forget and start again. But, God, when he exploded it wasn't usually *his* fault, it was hers – winding him up about something, pissing him off about this and that. Basically, she was a spoilt little girl and that kind of attitude needed to be knocked out of her, one way or the other. It was her parents' doing of course, they were to blame. How he loathed that overprotective mother of hers, always trying to poke her nose in, calling round unexpectedly with biscuits for the dog or some garment for Emily she'd found in a sale. And her father was just a plodding old twat who thought the sun shone out of his daughter's arse. Shit, he could tell them a thing or two about their angelic daughter that would blow their tiny minds! Why couldn't they just stay away from him and Emily, let them get on with it like his parents did? Then he could really turn Emily into an obedient little puppet – a puppet whose strings would get easier to pull with every week that passed.

"I didn't know Scott was leaving!" said Emily when Darren produced the sample scripts and asked her to come up with a new thirty second one for a double glazing company.

"Not many people do yet," he replied, "And with any luck the job won't need to be advertised… Lenny's quite happy for you to have a crack at it if you do a good job with this double glazing ad'. I said you'd give him a couple of promo' scripts too for all these Beach Party Roadshows we've got lined up. It's a piece of piss really…"

Emily quickly put pen to paper and mentally hugged herself with the happiness of this unexpected opportunity. Lenny was great; a nice family man and a respected producer with a long track record in the industry. She'd always got on well with him and was thrilled at the prospect of joining the Commercial Production team at Rocket. And fancy Darren putting her forward for it in the first place… he must really care about her to encourage such a wonderful opportunity. Things may even be better between them if she worked full time at Rocket – a proper job with a proper wage. They'd be work colleagues, comrades, with respect for each other's department and the work they both produced.

Two days later she sat down on Lenny's swivel chair as he leant up against the mixing desk and read through her work.

"Hah!" he said when he came to a witticism and "Like it…" when he approved of a certain play on words. "These are really good… *really* good and it saves us the bother of advertising to fill the post. What do you think? Fancy it? Glen says we can offer five quid a script and as you know we produce about a hundred a month all in all."

Emily hardly needed to be asked twice. This was it; the lucky break she'd been waiting for. She wasn't just a volunteer at Rocket any more – now she could really be someone, someone who mattered. "God, I'd love to do it! Of course I would! Thanks *so* much Lenny. When do I start?!"

Emily punched the security code into the keypad by the door handle and when the green light flashed on she burst into Engineering.

"I've got it! Lenny says I've got it! I'm the new Commercial Script Writer!"

The Assistant Engineer, Les, who was busy with a soldering iron and a complicated bunch of wires, looked up and smiled his approval.

"Excellent," said Darren, "I knew you'd get it.... Emily, this is Mel Green, she's just joined the Newsroom as a Senior Reporter. We used to work together at Radio City up in Manchester...."

Emily and Mel shook hands and exchanged pleasantries whilst Darren thought back several years to the times he'd fucked the excitable Mel. They'd met at a nightclub on New Year's Eve – Maxim's wasn't it? - that dreadful night when Davina had come along and made such a fool of herself and then gone and topped herself with that fatal dose of weed killer. Mel had been a trainee in the newsroom at Radio City and she'd steadily worked her way though every willing male at the station. Well, well, well... fancy Mel ending up here at Rocket Sound. Darren casually wondered if she'd be up for a threesome and if so how Emily would respond to the idea. He felt himself getting hard at the thought of it and forced his mind towards more mundane matters.

"Come on," he said to Emily, "Let's walk up to the pub for some lunch – celebrate your good news. Coming, Les? Mel?"

Emily walked up to the local pub with a spring in her step. Sitting in that smoky bar on a threadbare seat, eating chips and drinking lager, she let the tittle tattle conversation of station gossip wash over her. ... *Spilt coffee on the mixing desk, fucking twat... totally cocked up the two o'clock news bulletin... yes, someone's head in Sales is going to roll but don't say I said anything… talk about creative accounting… Pete's getting the graveyard slot? No way! Still, his latest figures were crap…* Emily nodded and smiled and chipped in with appropriately timed 'oohs' and 'ahs'. She was a part of this team, this exciting and respected team. She'd found a direction in life. She was Rocket Sound's new Commercial Script Writer and things could only get better.

Over the following weeks of the summer Emily and Darren got into a working routine. They drove to the station together every morning, dropping off Cocoa with Maria en route and collecting him again on the way home. Darren was vehemently wishing that he'd never bought the sodding dog now that it meant a trip to bloody Oakside Grange every day, and he set about persuading Emily to leave Cocoa with her parents during the week and just have him back home for the weekend. To his surprise Emily readily agreed. Her mum and dad adored Cocoa and were more than happy to have him but moreover Emily hated to see him cower and hide when Darren shouted at her. She would feel as sorry for Cocoa as she did for herself and was glad to put him in the safe and loving environment of Oakside. Unfortunately, this new routine of theirs still included the bickering, sulking and fighting that had become such a constant feature of their marriage. Darren had not physically hurt Emily again in the same way that he had drawn blood on their honeymoon but the threat of such an assault was always there below the surface. A sharp shove to the ground became common place as did a vicious pinch of the skin or a tug of the hair, and Emily was told so many times that she was 'nothing' without Darren that she began to believe it. Every hour of her existence was spent in proximity to Darren O'Dowel and she was becoming increasingly dependent on him to survive – or so she was being told.

"You need me," Darren would drum into her, "You need me because you can't stand on your own two feet without me! What kind of job would you have now if it wasn't for me, eh? Pulling pints probably! And where would you be living? I'll tell you where, shall I? Still at home with mummy and daddy – a spoilt baby with no chance of getting anywhere in life. God, you really do owe me everything, Emily, and don't you fucking forget it."

The End of Emily West

Emily's bruised ego would suffer a fresh blow after one of these frequent verbal assaults and the once so confident young lady would retreat further back into her shell. Darren never let her forget that he had 'got her the job' at Rocket Sound and always reinforced the notion that he could take it away from her too. Emily began to despise him for making these threats but always came back to the fact that she was too weak, useless and helpless to do anything about it. She had shrivelled up inside. Her resolve had the fragility of a dried out autumn leaf, seemingly robust yet in reality quite dead, needing only the strength of a child's hand to crush it to pieces. Darren O'Dowel became like a leech sucking the life blood out of its victim and Emily West hadn't got the strength left inside her to break free.

Emily had been at Rocket Sound for nearly six months when the incident happened which would result in her returning to Woolacombe in Devon. Who would have thought that an innocent comment on an ordinary Monday morning would have sparked off such a crashing series of events? It was a crisp and sunny day in early December and Emily nipped out of the car at Oakside Grange to drop off Cocoa there for the week. Darren sat fiddling with some cassette tapes and didn't start to turn the car around in the driveway until Emily climbed in again and shut the door. Maria stood in the doorway waving with one hand and holding onto Cocoa's collar with the other. Darren had been tense and irritable all weekend and Emily was glad to be heading to work, away from the strict confines of her home life with Darren. On the Friday Darren had been gratified to discover that as Chief Engineer he was being considered for an official 'Executive' position at Rocket Sound – a position that would place him in a managerial role of some importance.

"About time too," he had said to Emily but the tension of the situation had resulted in argument rather than celebration.

Emily wound down the car window and waved back to Maria shouting, "Bye, mum," and then at Cocoa, "Bye, my beautiful baby!"

Darren turned out of the driveway and joined the line of traffic which was making steady progress towards the town.

"*What?*" he said incredulously, mocking her previous words, "*Bye, my beautiful baby?* You've got a screw loose! Still, how like you to think more of a dumb dog than a *real* baby."

Emily stared straight ahead already feeling drained and deflated from the snide remark and desperate not to give Darren further reason to start a fight.

"What's up? Cat got your tongue?" Darren pushed.

"No, of course not. I just call Cocoa that sometimes, that's all..."

Darren reached over to turn down the radio and as *Careless Whisper* played softly in the background he ventured, "A dog isn't a substitute for a baby you know. Actually it's a subject I've been thinking quite a lot about recently... children... you getting pregnant..."

Emily cringed at his pompous delivery of the words, reminding her of the very few occasions she had come into contact with Albert. She imagined Darren sitting on his own in their kitchen late into the night, smoking joints and drinking whiskey, contemplating the conception and birth of his child, his heir. Were her thoughts or feelings considered or was Darren's precious seed the only thing of any value? Her jaw stiffened as she sensed trouble over this most hated subject. On the week of their honeymoon Emily had silently vowed never to have children. What a shitty depressing world she would be delivering a child into and how could she condemn it to having Darren O'Dowel as a father? She tried to think of something to say, something that would satisfy Darren for the moment yet was non-committal on the subject.

"Well, it's something to think about for the future," she lied. "Perhaps when I've got a bit more work under my belt..."

Darren laughed unkindly. "What has that got to do with anything? Surely you're not placing any great importance on your crappy scriptwriting job?"

"It's not crappy to me," said Emily quietly and indeed she thought that if she assessed her life as it stood at the moment, her work as Commercial Script Writer was the only thing which had any substance and meaning, the only thing she was praised and appreciated for, the only aspect of her being that she took any pride in.

The End of Emily West

They pulled up at some traffic lights and Darren stamped hard on the brakes as if to reinforce his argument.

"You will not use that job as an excuse for not getting pregnant," he shouted. "For fuck's sake you're an *amateur* just playing at being a script writer! You only got a fucking job because I pushed for it and they couldn't be arsed to advertise for someone better – don't you know that?"

Emily shrank away from his harsh words and from the finger he was pointing in her face. She looked out of her window and saw another driver staring at them. The protective shell of the car couldn't hide the fact that they were having a heated argument and she felt her face flush with embarrassment.

"Please stop it, Darren," she found herself pleading, "I am good at my job, I am. There's no way Lenny would keep me on if I wasn't doing well at it."

"God, you really do think a lot of yourself, don't you? If it wasn't for me being in a position of power at that poxy station they'd probably be thinking of replacing you by now. Think about that when you're busy putting off having my child. It's me you should be fucking loyal to, not them."

Darren rambled on with a tirade of insults and accusations and as they turned into the road which was home to Rocket Sound Emily gave up trying to stop the tears from falling. He'd taken her personal life already, he'd stamped her into the ground and had made her scared of her own shadow. And now he wanted her work too. It wasn't enough that he dominated and criticised her in every aspect of their domestic life together – now he wanted to undermine her confidence in her work, grind her down until she was so unsure of her own abilities and position in the station hierarchy that she would succumb to his wish and become nothing more than satisfactory breeding stock. Anger and misery were burning inside her. She was totally trapped. Darren had made her believe that she could not survive without him. Without Darren she didn't have a home... she'd have to go back to Oakside Grange with her tail between her legs. And how could she live there again like a little girl when she had become so reliant on dope, cigarettes and whiskey to help her limp through the chore of existing? And what about her job? That too was all part and parcel of being married to Darren O'Dowel. In short, the strength that would be required to extract herself from this situation was a force she simply did not possess. But she knew **one** thing with a deadly certainty – she would rather die than have Darren's baby.

Darren parked the car at the back of the station by the entrance which led into the Engineering Department. He tore the keys from the ignition and turned to face Emily, gripping her lower thigh with such viciousness it made her wince and cry out in pain.

"I'll teach you," he hissed, "I'll teach you what it means to be obedient."

"I don't want to have your children, Darren," she screamed back at him, "I shall never have your children!"

She fled from the car into the station, not going straight to her little computer room as she usually did but finding sanctuary in the ladies' toilet. Her heart was racing – she could feel it heavy and pulsating in her chest - a frightened heart, sick in the knowledge that there would be a price to pay for her outburst.

After about ten minutes she rechecked her face in the mirror. Did her eyes look less puffy now? If someone from Sales came down to her with a script to write would they be able to tell she'd been crying? She tried to push aside all thoughts of what it would be like going home with Darren that night, of the path their argument would take if it continued, as it inevitably would. A voice-over artist was due in the next morning and she had a busy day ahead, mainly finishing off four scripts she'd started on Friday and clearing the copy with the respective clients. She had to keep her head down this morning and get on with her work. The little mouse had to put on a brave face – a happy, smiley mask which had done such a sterling job for her over the last year, fooling just about everyone she came into contact with.

When she opened the door to the glorified broom cupboard which she was proud to call 'her office', she knew immediately that something was wrong. The computer was on. The computer was on when she had most definitely turned it off on Friday night – switched it off after doing the bulk of the work on those four new scripts… the ones she hadn't bothered to print out because she trusted that they would be safely stored on the hard drive. Emily peered at the screen as the full horror and panic of what was happening flooded over her. A note was lying on the keyboard, 'Please come and see me in Engineering, Darren.' Of course it was him who had done this to her. Who else would take satisfaction in losing every single thing that was stored in the computer's memory by deliberately formatting the hard drive?

Emily felt sick with dread at the thought of redoing the work she had lost in time for the voice-over session tomorrow. And the bitterness she felt towards Darren curled and twisted and knotted inside her as she conceded defeat. She had thought she was someone who mattered here at Rocket Sound, a valued member of the team. But Darren was a Head of Department, almost an executive manager and it was obvious where the station's loyalties would lie if she dared to tell anyone what Darren had just done to her computer. She was good at what she did but she was also easily replaceable. She wanted to hide in her little room and never come out but she forced herself to walk down the windowless corridor to Engineering. Better for her to go to him that to wait for him to come charging along to her. And in any case she had no idea how to get the computer working again without Darren's help. Darren was right – she couldn't stand on her own two feet, she needed him to survive. How she dreaded the next few minutes… but what if he was already regretting what he'd done. What if he was sitting there in Engineering mortified at the severity of his actions, waiting for the chance to put things right. Maybe her work could be saved. She didn't know. To her the computer was just a supped up typewriter. She didn't understand the technology like Darren did. *Please let Darren be sorry for what he's done. Please let him be nice to me.*

Emily punched the security code into the key pad and opened the door. Les had his nose buried in some manual and Darren was leaning back in his chair sipping coffee. He looked up as Emily came in.

"About time we changed that security code, Les, don't you think?"

Les glanced up, embarrassed, taken unaware by the obvious implied insult. He shifted uncomfortably in his seat and turned his attention back to his book, pretending to be too engrossed in its pages to get involved in a discussion about new security codes.

Emily stood there, wanting the ground to swallow her up and suffocate her. She croaked out, "The computer…"

Darren rolled his eyeballs and gave and exaggerated sigh. "Oh dear, crashed has it? Do I have to come to your rescue, yet again?" And he propelled her out of the doorway back down the corridor.

When they got to her office and Darren closed the door behind them Emily sat on her swivel chair and cried out, "What am I going to do?"

She pushed her fists into her eyes and wished the darkness she found there could last forever. Knowing that it couldn't made her want to take the easier option of drowning herself in a bottle of whiskey.

"What you're going to do," said Darren, "Is to sit here all day and catch up on the work you profess to be so fucking good at. Then what you're going to do is learn to be subservient and not the piss poor excuse for a wife you are at the moment."

Emily sat in silence whilst Darren's fingers flew across the computer keyboard. It was ready to use again, but all her previous work was lost forever.

Darren walked out without a backward glance and didn't see Emily for the rest of the day. By six o'clock Emily had rewritten Friday's scripts and started and finished two more. They weren't her best efforts but they were good enough to go on air and do the job required of them. She hadn't eaten all day and had only kept going because of the nervous energy provided by plenty of coffee and a copy deadline. She turned off her computer, picked up her coat and went towards Engineering to find Darren. They always left together between six and half past although Emily often thought it would be lovely to have a car of her own. She hoped and prayed that Darren had calmed down and that the business of the day had diluted his feelings of anger towards her. As she reached Engineering Les was coming out, turning off the lights and producing a set of car keys from his pocket.

"Oh Les," she said breezily, "Is Darren not in there? Perhaps he's upstairs in the boardroom…"

Once again Les found himself in an awkward situation and he silently cursed Darren O'Dowel for having put him there.

"Well, er… the fact is he left at about four. Perhaps he left a message for you and you didn't get it…"

Emily tried to cover her bewilderment. "Oh, yes… of course, that's probably what's happened… I'll just have to hop on the bus…"

Her happy, smiley mask didn't fool Les for a minute and he wondered, as most of the station staff did, what the hell Emily West was doing with a merciless bastard like Darren O'Dowel.

"Don't be daft," he said, not giving her the opportunity to object, "I can easily give you a lift home. Come on."

They made small talk for the fifteen minute duration of the journey. Emily knew Les felt sorry for her which made her feel young and silly and totally humiliated. She was keen to get home – keen to escape from the well-meaning Les and desperate to numb her pain with a tumbler full of whiskey. How Darren would behave towards her that evening remained to be seen.

Chapter 27

EMILY LET HERSELF INTO THE HOUSE and went straight to the kitchen to pour herself a drink. A glance through to the living room told her that Darren was already drinking and the room was thick with tobacco smoke and the heavy smell of dope. She sat at the kitchen table taking big mouthfuls of the whiskey and ginger ale, wondering what to do for the best. Should she go into the living room and try to win Darren round? Should she dress up for him like the girls in his porn magazines and try to buy his affection with sex? Would he rather be left on his own, and if so should she sneak up to the bedroom now with her glass and the whiskey bottle?

She was still going over her options when Darren appeared in the kitchen.

"Hello," she said. "I didn't know you were leaving early today... it was alright though – Les gave me a lift back..."

"Oh yes? Did he try it on with you?"

"No! He doesn't fancy me! Anyway, Les respects you too much to even think of doing such a thing."

"Oh, does he fuck! He's just an underhand little prick like all the rest of you."

The End of Emily West

Emily could see the way the evening was going, although thanks to the whiskey it was getting nicely fuzzy around the edges. Ironically though the alcohol always loosened her tongue and it was when this gave her the false confidence to bite back that she always came off worse. She drained her glass and poured another before making her way into the living room to roll a joint. She sat down on the settee and set about the task in hand on the coffee table in front of her. Darren came in eventually with his own glass refreshed and sat in the arm chair opposite her. Emily glanced up to find him staring at her intently, his cold black eyes never flickering away for a second. She took a long deep drag at the finished joint and felt compelled to say something to break the awful silence.

"What are you thinking about?" she asked. Perhaps she could do something to bring him out of this terrible mood.

"Not much. Just wondering what you'd look like with no hair. If I shaved off your pubes and all the hair on your head so that you were completely bald, I wonder if that would really turn me on?"

Emily tried to reply with a throwaway laugh but it stuck in her throat. "You're joking…" she managed. She looked into his eyes but realised that although they were looking directly back at her they were glazed over. He was sitting there, smouldering. A white heat was burning up inside him and he became like coiled spring, ready to pounce. Emily didn't know what to do or what to say. All she did know was that Darren was coldly assessing her potential, wondering whether she'd make a good subject for his newly thought up sex game. She also knew that he wasn't joking. She got up from the settee and pushed past the coffee table.

"I think I'd better go up to bed," she said.

In a split second he was on her, knocking her to the ground and kicking her in the stomach. She cried and screamed and curled herself up into a ball.

"Beg for forgiveness," he shouted at her, spitting out the words like a venomous snake. "Don't want my children? *Don't want my fucking children?* Beg me for fucking forgiveness! Beg me, you stuck up little bitch, *beg, beg, beg*!"

Emily cried and pleaded and begged for Darren to forgive her. He stopped kicking her and stumbled over to the fireplace, taking ornaments from the mantelpiece and throwing them down at her one by one. Glass and china rained down. One or two pieces bounced off Emily and remained intact whilst the majority shattered against the wall or the coffee table before showering her with their broken remains. She stayed huddled up on the floor whilst Darren smashed his way through the room. Eventually he stopped and drank greedily from a bottle of whiskey. Emily's sobs and cries had turned into nothing more than a petrified whimper as she lay frozen on the carpet with her hands over her head. Darren sat down heavily on the settee, almost panting with the effort of his rage. He rolled himself a joint and drank more whiskey. Emily had no idea how long she had stayed down on the carpet in the same foetal position but when eventually she dared to look up Darren's head was back against a cushion and his eyes were closed.

Emily stared at the scene of destruction – so many beautiful things broken at the hands of her husband. Many of the items they had been given as wedding presents lay in pieces on the carpet, and a piece of old Moorcroft pottery that had belonged to Emily's grandma was damaged beyond repair. Emily imagined her grandma buying the vase when it was brand new, spotting it in a shop window. A different age, a different life. *What a wonderful vase… that vivid blue will go perfectly in our front room.* Years later it had been passed onto Maria and years after that it had been given to Emily. It had survived all this time because it had been loved and cherished by its owners. Now, in a spilt second, Darren O'Dowel had taken it and destroyed it without a second thought.

Emily rose to her feet, wincing at the pain in her stomach and ribs. The telephone started ringing and when the answer machine clicked in she could hear Mr Johnson's voice, wondering when she was next coming to Whitemoor Farm. Crunching over shards of broken treasures she made her way out of the room and progressed slowly up the stairs and into their bedroom. Lying on the bed, staring up at the ceiling, her head still foggy with drink and shock, she came to the conclusion that there was no point in wishing she was dead as to all intent and purposes she was dead already. She heard a knock on the front door. After a minute whoever it was knocked again. Then there was silence. Some time later she drifted off into an uneasy, drink-induced sleep.

When the ice-cold water hit Emily's face it woke her up with a sharpness that made her scream out in horror and confusion. Darren was standing over her with a bucket, empting its cold contents on her until she lay crying in a soggy tangle of clothes and bed sheets. He grabbed her forearm and yanked her up off the bed.

"How dare you walk away from me!" he thundered, "I'm going to fucking kill you!"

His two hands closed around Emily's neck and he pushed his thumbs against her throat.

"*Beg me* not to kill you. *Beg me* to let you live."

Emily coughed and spluttered out the words he was demanding to hear until his hands started to relax their grip. But she knew her ordeal wasn't over. He grabbed a fist full of her hair and pulled her towards the bedroom door.

"Get downstairs and clean up that fucking mess."

Once down the stairs Emily dutifully scampered into the kitchen to find a bin bag and a dustpan and brush. Then she went into the living room and began the soul destroying job of clearing away the ornaments and pictures which lay broken and ruined on the floor. It was half past ten. Darren watched her work from the comfort of the settee, a never ending drink in one hand and a joint in the other. Eventually, as before, his head fell back against the cushions and he fell fast asleep. When Emily had finished cleaning up the room, she curled up on the arm chair with a large glass of whiskey and ginger ale with the specific intention of drinking her way to sleep. At around midnight she got what she wanted.

Mr Johnson cleared his throat nervously when he realised Emily wasn't going to pick up the 'phone. He hated talking to that silly answering machine.

"Oh, er, hello Emily... just ringing up for a chat and to let you know the farrier can't come 'til Wednesday week. Haven't seen you for a while. Still, I know how busy you are. See your mum and dad of course every day... feeding and grooming Rascal – you'd think they'd had horses all their lives! Anyways… hope you're enjoying this cold weather. No good for my joints I can tell you that. See you soon then. Oh, and Mrs Johnson sends her love. Bye then. Bye."

Mr Johnson replaced the receiver and thought back to the last time Emily had been over to groom Rascal, a couple of weeks ago. She'd looked so drained and pale. Mrs Johnson said she'd lost all her sparkle since marrying that Darren chap. What was that all about ever? He was so much older than her and the one time he'd come down to the stables they hadn't taken to him at all. Where was that little girl, Mr Johnson wondered, who used to come bounding into the yard ready to practice show jumping and gymkhana games at the top of the field. Where on earth had she gone?

Jackie Dean knocked on Emily and Darren's front door. Darren's car was in the driveway so she assumed they were in. Well, hopefully only Emily was at home and not Darren. She had thought he was a real dick head when they'd first met at that summer Roadshow and he'd given her no reason since to change her opinion. He was so smug and condescending and any fool could see how he undermined Emily's confidence. She was still married to him though, wasn't she? Emily must think the sun shone out of his backside so who was she to try and tell her otherwise? Jackie knocked once more but still no one answered. The thought suddenly occurred to Jackie that maybe Emily and Darren were in bed. They were probably in the full throws of passion and were cursing whoever it was who was persistently knocking on their front door. She gave up and climbed back into her car. She had only been passing anyway and thought she'd pop in and tell Emily about her new fella. They'd met two days ago and she was dying to tell someone all the details of her latest conquest. Oh well, as far as telling Emily was concerned it would obviously have to wait.

Mel Green sat waiting for some friends to join her in the Sword and Dragon. She was relaxed and contented, unfazed by the fact she was sitting in a pub on her own. She was half way through her second bottle of lager and exuded all the glow and confidence of someone who has recently had sex. Fancy bumping in Darren O'Dowel again. Still, the radio industry was a small world and people's paths were constantly crossing as they fought their way up the chain of command. When she'd bumped into Darren outside Studio One at three thirty that afternoon she couldn't resist a little flirt for old times sake. Darren had been in a sharp, almost aggressive mood and had almost demanded that she find an excuse to leave the newsroom at four o'clock and meet him in his car further down the road. She had expected a continuation of their flirtatious conversation and was favourably impressed when he slammed the car into gear and sped off towards his home. Mel was young, free and single without a care in the world. She revelled in this kind of dangerous sexual adventure and didn't give two shits about the fact that Darren was married. That silly little cow Emily obviously wasn't giving a man like Darren the kind of sex he needed or he wouldn't be turning to her for it, would he? She put the bottle of Pils up to her lips and took a long swig. Luckily Darren had wanted it fast and furious that afternoon… Mel didn't mind shagging a married man but she didn't particularly need the hassle of wifey coming home and walking in on them. She wondered what Darren was up to this evening and laughed inwardly… he would be too worn out to fuck Emily, that much was for sure.

Maria was sitting on the settee reading the local paper whilst William was flicking idly through the Radio Times.

"Oh," said Maria, "Look what's on at The Playhouse… A Christmas Carol! I'd love to see that this year. I wonder if Emily would like to come..?"

"Sounds good," said William, "Why don't you ask her? You could see the play and go and have dinner somewhere afterwards."

Maria lowered the paper and thought through all the ramifications of the idea. Now it didn't seem like such a good suggestion after all.

"Yes… but at the end of the day I suppose it'll be easier to ask Fiona if she fancies it. Emily hasn't wanted to do the last few things I've suggested. *'Is Darren invited?'* That's what she always asks and quite frankly I'd rather not go at all than to put up with him all night. God, it's like they're joined at the hip!"

"When will she come to her senses?" William said suddenly.

"I don't know," said Maria, "I honestly thought she'd have left him by now… you know, realised that the whole thing was a huge mistake."

"All we can do is be here for her when she needs us," said William, trotting out their much used philosophy on the matter, "It's like we've always said – she'd not a little girl anymore."

Maria went back to her paper, reading the words but not taking them in. Emily would *always* be her little girl and she hated Darren O'Dowel with a passion for taking her away.

Paul Andrew stood under the shower in his family's Sydney home and contemplated his forthcoming trip back to England. An ancient, long forgotten aunty had surprised them all by leaving a large part of her estate to Paul and the solicitor had advised him to fly back and sign off on the relevant documents. After all these years away it would be great to catch up with some of his old friends… and Emily. All those daft promises he'd made about going back as soon as he was able… a romantic and noble ideal but they'd only been kids, hadn't they? He could never have known back then how easily he and his parents would have settled here in Sydney. He could never have guessed how quickly he would get caught up in the whirlwind of his new life, consigning his past to nothing more than a sweet and distant memory. His sixteenth birthday came and went and the time had just slipped away. He'd been shocked to receive a letter from Emily telling him of her wedding plans. His stomach had tightened with the memories of the times they'd spent together. Him, Emily and Karen Black… 'The Three Musketeers' she had called them once when they'd shared a picnic tea one cloudless sunny day at Whitemoor Farm. Happy days. He wondered what Emily was doing at this moment. It would be mid evening back in England. Perhaps she was having a romantic dinner with that husband of hers. Paul felt slightly tortured by this thought and suddenly found himself in a quandary regarding his visit to England which was scheduled for the New Year. Should he make a point of seeing Emily? Or would it be easier to attend to the business he was specifically visiting for and slip quietly away? The thought of seeing Emily again made him feel nervous, and as yet he couldn't quite pinpoint the reason why.

The End

Chapter 28

❦

"OH CHRIST, NO! OH, EMILY... EMILY, what have I done?"

Emily woke up to find Darren on his knees beside her chair, imploring her to forgive him and start afresh.

"Fucking hell... Oh shit... I can't think what came over me... you'd made me so mad... so angry... you're always undermining me... putting me down. I just got out of control... you know I don't want to hurt you Emily... please believe me... *please*. Let's start again... let's forget all this ever happened and start again...say we can start again Emily, please..."

Darren's watery eyes confirmed to Emily that this time he really was sorry and that this time they really would put all the nastiness behind them and start again. Why did she make him so mad? What kind of a person was she that she could induce someone to behave like Darren did? It was going to be alright. Darren loved her; he was sitting here now and telling her so over and over again. He'd had far too much to drink and she'd pushed him over the edge. That and the fact that he was feeling the tension about this possible managerial post at Rocket Sound.

"I was so fucked off when you said you didn't want children... I'll give you some more time... I'll *prove* to you that I can be a good father... and don't you see, Emily? If you were carrying my child there's no way I'd lay a finger on you, is there? It'd almost be like insurance… you'd be completely safe…."

The words washed over Emily and she knew that what she was hearing was wrong; that she shouldn't have to be pregnant in order to guarantee her safety. It didn't matter. For at this moment in time she was simply happy enough that the violence had stopped and Darren was being nice to her. She so desperately wanted to believe that married life could be good that she was prepared to deceive herself into thinking just that. She looked at her watch and saw that it was eight o'clock.

"I'm going to ring work," said Darren, "Say that we've both got some kind of virus and won't be in today."

Once Darren had made the call to Rocket Sound he led Emily up to the spare bedroom where they both slept until early afternoon. Emily woke first and in those first few seconds of consciousness wondered what on earth they were doing in the spare room. Then she remembered. She swung her legs over the side of the bed and crept out. Her limbs ached and she felt tired and lethargic. The skin on her face felt dry and grubby, like dirty parchment, and her hair was a knotted, unattractive mess of blonde. Her stomach felt sore and closer examination revealed a collection of angry bruises. She went over to their bed and stared for a moment at the still sodden mattress and bed linen. How calm and quiet everything was now, this afternoon, in the cold winter daylight. How different to the screaming and shouting, the pain and humiliation of the night before. Slowly, methodically, she began to strip the bed. The mattress could begin to dry out whilst she gave the sheets and pillow cases a wash through.

With her arms full of soaking sheets she stopped en route to the kitchen to look into the lounge. It stank of stale tobacco and forgotten dregs of whiskey. The room was cold and depressing. There was nothing cosy about it, nothing warm or welcoming. It was a sparse and shameful reminder of what had gone on the night before and Emily sobbed into the wet sheets as she remembered all those lovely objects which were now consigned to the bin. And what if her mum made one of those dreaded unannounced visits? How was she going to explain away all those missing things? Chips of china and tiny shards of glass were still embedded in the carpet and once Emily had set the washer going she took out the vacuum cleaner and swept the living room floor.

The noise of it must have disturbed Darren because by the time she had finished he was trotting down the stairs. Unlike Emily, Darren seemed to have boundless energy and he was almost falling over his words with enthusiasm for his latest idea. He sat down on the settee and beckoned her to sit beside him as he laid out his plan.

"We need a break. We need to get away from this fucking place and that fucking radio station. We're going away for the weekend. I've worked it all out. As soon as we've finished work on Thursday we're going to drive down to Cornwall. We'll try and get off early. I haven't been to Cornwall for years. What about Newquay? You've been to Newquay before haven't you?"

"Devon… it was Woolacombe in Devon… near Ilfracombe."

"Yeah, that's right, Woolacombe Bay. Let's head for there and just stay wherever we like the look of. No need to book anything in advance. We need some time alone, don't we? Just the two of us, away from all this shit – away from Rocket and this house and your parents. Christ, how many times are they going to ask us over for Sunday lunch?! Don't they get the message? We don't *need* them. We don't *want* them interfering in our lives…"

Darren's diatribe went on and on and on and as it did so Emily forced herself to look at his face and assess her feelings for him. She no longer loved him, but she had known that for a long time. She had done once, or she thought she had. Now she feared him; feared his presence and his temper. And worst of all she loathed herself for not having the strength of character to do anything about it. Would he ever change? Could she still sit here and dare to hope that Darren would ever become a warm, compassionate, loving man - that one day all this time she had invested in their relationship would be rewarded? What other option was there when she was so mentally weak, so ground down by him that all she could do was follow meekly behind him, taking whichever path he deemed they should take. His eyes had dark circles beneath them and today Darren was showing every year of the fifteen year age gap. His skin was pasty and dull and he had the first signs of a receding hairline and a double chin. Had these things been evident before or had they suddenly come into being today? Of course, Emily knew the answer. They had been there for some time but she had chosen not to see them. Darren O'Dowel was an unattractive person in every sense and she had only just begun to allow herself to admit it. If he had been a 'catch' at one time, he wasn't now. If he'd been amusing and dashing and charming at one time, he wasn't now. Emily imagined being his partner for the rest of her life. The thought instantly gave her that familiar feeling of wanting to go to sleep and never wake up.

At three o'clock that Thursday afternoon Emily sat beside Darren in the car, heading south towards Devon with a feeling of utter dread. Why had she let him talk her into going? It was freezing cold, wet and windy – the weather reflecting her mood perfectly. She had no desire to go away for the weekend and no desire to be so very alone with Darren. She was nervous and jumpy and hadn't been able to eat any lunch on account of it. She had to focus on one thing, that was all she kept telling herself – just concentrate on keeping Darren happy. Be nice to him, agree with him, pander to him. Just get through this weekend so they could get back home. Back home to what? She didn't know and didn't care. All she did know was that the prospect of a weekend alone with her husband made her feel vulnerable and afraid. And what did she feel about returning to Woolacombe? She'd spent the last two days trying not to think about it, but now it could hardly be avoided. Darren reached over and put a tape of Blondie's Parallel Lines into the car's cassette player. Emily leaned her head back against the seat as Debbie Harry punched out, *'I'm in the 'phone booth, it's the one across the hall!'* Darren knew it was one of Emily's favourite albums. He thumped the top of the steering wheel to the beat of the music.

"I'm really looking forward to this!" he said and he looked at Emily and smiled.

She smiled back at him. Perhaps it wouldn't be such a bad weekend after all.

By the time they reached the outskirts of Ilfracombe at half past eight that night Darren was tired and irritable and had completely lost his previous spirit of adventure. Emily was keeping her eyes peeled for a suitable place to stay, not daring to suggest to Darren that they should really have booked somewhere up in advance. A fair number of the Bed and Breakfast houses were closed to customers for the winter and one which was open and had looked really pretty a couple of streets back had a notice in the front window saying 'no vacancies'. Darren cursed and swore as they drove around the empty avenues and dark back streets. He hadn't thought to buy a map of the area and was pissed off with driving around in what seemed like circles.

"Look!" said Emily suddenly, "What about that guest house called The Dunes? That looks alright...."

They parked up outside The Dunes and knocked on the front door. It was a substantial Victorian property in a row of others and a large Christmas tree stood proudly in the front bay window. The salt wind from the sea whipped around them, stinging any exposed skin and once again Emily questioned the wisdom of visiting a seaside town in the middle of winter. Seaside towns were for summer holidays when it was dry and warm and you could sit on the beach eating ice cream and building sand castles. They were for families, like the one she used to belong to.

Presently, the front door to The Dunes opened and an elderly gentleman in blue cord trousers and a thick grey jumper stood before them, inviting them in. Darren booked a room for the next three nights. Looking around, Emily could tell that The Dunes had seen better days. The colour scheme was confused and old fashioned and the furniture was an unappealing hotch potch of old and new. Still, it was clean and warm and the owner, Mr Croft, showed them to a large double bedroom featuring a television along with tea making facilities. There was no en-suite; just a washbasin in the corner and a shared bathroom along with hall. Darren opened up the windows and the full impact of the winter night invaded the room.

"We don't want that old codger complaining about the smell of dope, do we?" he smirked.

Emily agreed and pulled her coat more tightly around her body, blocking out the freezing air. She wondered what normal couples did in this kind of situation. In a normal life she wouldn't be sitting on the edge of the bed, cold and tired, smoking joints and pouring whiskey into coffee cups. She and her husband would be laughing at the dated furnishings and the bouncy bed, snuggling up together to watch a film on the TV and making plans for the weekend. But Emily no longer had any illusions that this was a normal relationship. This sham of a marriage was her guilty secret – hers to endure and hers to hide from the world.

The following day brought a misty drizzle although the forecast for the Saturday was at least dry, if cold. When they overslept and eventually went downstairs at nine fifteen, Mrs Croft had no qualms about telling them that they had missed breakfast.

"Breakfast finishes at nine o'clock on the dot," she informed them. "Sorry, no exceptions or I'd find myself spending all morning in the kitchen!"

Emily wasn't particularly bothered. She'd been a vegetarian for a few years now and didn't crave 'a full English' in the same way Darren did. In any case she was pretty sure that Mr Croft had mentioned the nine o'clock cut off point the night before.

"Fucking old bag!" Darren exploded as he stormed ahead of Emily out of The Dunes. Emily trotted after him, desperately hoping that Mrs Croft hadn't heard Darren's description of her. The day had got off to a bad start and now she'd have to walk on egg shells in an effort to get it back on track.

They drove into the centre of Ilfracombe and tried to ignore the miserable weather as they walked around the town. Emily vaguely recognised some bits of it and was shocked to find herself turn a corner and be suddenly accosted by the memory of visiting Mr Platt's jewellery shop with her mum. She looked down at the ring Maria had bought for her that day; the ring she had left on the beach at Woolacombe, the ring the Bobby had found by some 'miracle' in the sand the following morning. But when she looked up again and her eyes searched the street she couldn't see Mr Platt's shop. They walked on a little further and then it dawned on Emily what had happened. It was quite simple really... Mr Platt's Jewellery Emporium did not exist anymore. The proud sign, that beautiful window display, the front door with the old fashioned bell which rang as a customer came or went had vanished. And in its place was an 'Everything For A Pound' shop.

They ambled around the town – Emily still shocked at the demise of the Jewellery Emporium and Darren getting increasingly irritable. Emily irritated him, the weather irritated him, Mrs Croft irritated him… bloody stupid idea of Emily's to come to this God forsaken place. He led the way into the off licence to stock up on drink and cigarettes. Should they go out for a meal tonight? Christ, he wasn't *made* of money and Emily hardly deserved it. She could have a bag of chips and be bloody grateful.

※

She should never have come back. What a fool she had been to ever come back. She had known it yesterday whilst staring in disbelief at the 'pound shop' and she knew it now as Darren swung the car into the car park at Woolacombe beach. Darren switched off the engine and she began to panic. She was about to visit the past and she had absolutely no desire to do so, not with Darren, not like this.

"Perhaps we should carry on around the coast for a bit," she said. "I'm really not bothered about going onto this beach in particular…"

"Of course you're bothered!" replied Darren, "You went on and on about it once – this bloody marvellous beach and your perfect family holiday – of course you're fucking *bothered*. And I haven't driven all this frigging way for nothing you know. Now let's go and see it then we can get to the pub for some lunch."

Emily felt the familiar sting of tears along with bitter frustration welling up inside her. Who was this monster who didn't give a shit about her feelings? And how had he managed to turn her into a frightened mouse who didn't dare to fight back?

They walked down onto the sand and Emily braced herself as she looked up and took in the full glory of the bay. Of course nothing had changed. The sea might be grey and the winter waves more fierce, but essentially nothing had changed. The sweep of glorious clean sand went on for miles, just as it had always done, and the row of beach huts still stood in a line by the dunes. The patch of sand and rocks that they had made their own all those years ago still remained and the gulls still swooped and cried as they battled against the wind.

"Christ," Darren said eventually, "It's fucking freezing!"

Emily agreed that it was, although in truth she hadn't noticed. She was too lost in her thoughts to feel the cold. Suddenly the years had been stripped away and it was the summer of '76 again. Her mum and dad were setting out a picnic on the sand, she was fishing a mermaid's purse out of a heap of seaweed and Bobby was throwing bread crusts to the sea gulls. Then she and Bobby were running off down the beach, holding hands, teasing each other with stories of sand monsters and sea witches. The memories were so vivid and painful that Emily had to physically stop her legs from buckling underneath her.

"What's up with you?" asked Darren. "We're meant to be having fun and all you've done so far is mope about."

"I never wanted to come back."

"*What?*"

Emily looked up at him and shouted, "I said, I never wanted to come back!"

Angry tears blinded her as she started to run across the beach back towards the car park. She was glad she couldn't see properly, glad that Woolacombe beach was such a blur that she couldn't take one more look at its December bleakness. She didn't want to remember it like this. She only wanted it to be a happy, sunny place – the last place that the four of them had been so happy together.

She stood by the car for several minutes before Darren came into view. She was dreading his return and wondered how she had found the courage for such an outburst. Previous experience had taught her that she would pay for such a thing. He reached the car and unlocked it, enabling both of them to climb in.

"God, you really know how to spoil things, don't you?" he began.

Emily stared ahead of her out of the window. The wind had started to howl around the car and in spite of the forecast raindrops appeared on the windscreen.

"I'm sorry," she whispered.

"Oh, you're always fucking sorry! Well I'll tell you this for nothing – you *will* be sorry, you will be *very* sorry!"

He started the car and rammed it into gear before spinning the wheels on the gravel and speeding out of the car park. Emily didn't know where they were going and didn't dare ask. Some way down the road Darren registered that it was raining and put the wipers on to clear the window. Emily was immediately treated to a clear and unmistakable view of the cottage called Tide's Reach. They sped past it and Emily twisted herself around to watch it grow smaller in the distance. At the next bend in the road it had vanished from sight. She turned back and kept her eyes focussed on the road ahead. She didn't want to think about Tide's Reach but her resolve was weak. Who was living there now? Was it a family home or was it still being let out to holiday makers? And in the bedroom which overlooked the garden, were the messages which she and Bobby had written on the floorboards still there?

Emily had half thought that Darren would take them back to The Dunes so they could pack up and leave immediately. She was surprised therefore when he eventually pulled over outside a country pub.

"You're not going to ruin *my* day," he said petulantly. "I'm going to have lunch and a drink. You can come in or stay here in the car. Please yourself."

Emily was hungry but above all wanted a large whiskey and ginger in an effort to start blocking out the pain of the day so far. With that in mind she followed Darren into the lounge bar of The Green Man.

They ate and drank in silence. The open log fire held no magic and the Christmas decorations which gaily adorned the bar only served to remind Emily that another stressful period – the festive season - was just around the corner. They drove back to The Dunes in silence although by now Emily's feelings of fear and trepidation had been dulled by the lunchtime whiskey. Darren stopped at an off license to buy more supplies of whiskey and ginger and as soon as they got into their room Emily set about pouring them drinks whilst Darren opened up the windows and rolled a large joint. The light outside was beginning to fade and Emily could see fairy lights being turned on in several houses along the street. She wondered what it must be like to actively look forward to Christmas; to be young and in love and actually *look forward* to entering that winter wonderland. She wasn't looking forward to it, she knew that much. She didn't look forward to anything anymore and the realisation made her start to cry.

Darren tutted and muttered under his breath, "For God's sake," before finally smashing down his cup on the dressing table and shouting, "Fucking hell! Why do you always have to spoil everything? You're a crap excuse for a wife! You'd still rather be living at home with mummy and daddy, tied to their fucking apron strings. I need someone more mature, more worldly, someone without all your pathetic emotional baggage. You're dragging me down, you can see that, can't you? You're holding me back...."

"You bastard! I hate you, I hate you, I hate you!" Emily sprang towards Darren like a wild cat and, taken totally off guard, he fell back against the dressing table, knocking his head on the mirror which then clattered to the floor.

The whiskey spoke as she clawed at his face. "Yes, I'd rather be living with them than with you. I hate you! You're old and fat and ugly and I'd rather fucking die before I had any children with you, you horrible mean bastard…"

Darren punched her on the side of her head and she fell away from him back onto the bed. She tried to get up but it was too late, Darren was on top of her in an instant with his hands squeezed around her throat.

"I should have killed you a long time ago, shouldn't I?" he hissed, spitting the words in her face.

Someone was hammering at the door.

"What's going on in there? What's going on?" It was Mrs Croft, alerted by all the shouting and the noise of the mirror falling from the wall.

Darren put his hand over Emily's mouth. "It's alright… nothing's going on. It's alright in here…"

"Well… I'd be obliged if you'd keep the noise down then…" And Mrs Croft shuffled back down the stairs.

"Now, *beg* me not to kill you," Darren shouted in her ear, "*Beg me*."

Emily began to beg as Darren's slaps and punches rained down on her. "Please Darren, please…"

"I don't think you'll ever learn to be obedient, will you? You'll never learn to serve me properly, will you?

Darren began to smack her head from side to side and Emily began to scream. After a final vicious blow to her ribs he got off her and snatched up his car keys, pushing past Mr and Mrs Croft who were now both standing outside the door ready to force their way in. Emily was distraught. What had she done? Darren was going but where would that leave her? Darren had become her life… she depended on him… her life revolved around him and her job at Rocket Sound was only safe while Darren wanted it to be. Where would she go? What would she do without him?

She cried out, "Darren, please don't leave me…"

Darren glanced back briefly with the parting shot, "I may come back to you one day if I need my shirts ironing."

The front door banged to as he left The Dunes and for a moment Mr and Mrs Croft simply stared at Emily in disbelief. Nothing like this had ever happened at The Dunes before.

Mrs Croft was the first to rally round.

"Oh, good gracious, my poor dear," she began, going over to Emily. "Raymond, call the police!"

"No!" Emily croaked, "Please…"

"Perhaps she's right," said Raymond, hideously embarrassed at the scene in which he found himself, "I'm sure we don't want any trouble…"

"Well, we have to do something," said Mrs Croft. "Come down to the kitchen, then we can call someone for you… someone who can come and collect you?"

Emily clung onto Mrs Croft as they both rose from the bed. "Yes… my mum and dad. Can you ring my mum and dad? I want my mum and dad."

A combination of dope, whiskey and Darren's assault made Emily stumble and fall as she held on to Mrs Croft, her saviour. When they finally reached the kitchen Raymond set about making some tea whilst Mrs Croft dialled the number Emily had given her for Maria and William. *They'll think I'm stupid* she thought, *they'll think I've failed.*

After Mrs Croft had given a brief explanation of events to William, along with the full address of The Dunes, she handed over the 'phone to Emily.

"Emily?"

"Oh, Dad…"

"Now listen to me, love. I want you to go to bed and try and get some rest, and mum and I are going to set off straightaway. If we get a good run we should be down there before midnight and Mrs Croft has promised to stay up so she can let us in. Then we're all going to stay the night and tomorrow we're going to bring you home."

"I want to come home, Dad…"

"I know you do, sweetheart. Mum and I are on our way."

Mrs Croft made Emily drink two cups of sweet tea before escorting her upstairs to lie down. Drained, aching and still rather drunk, Emily pulled the blanket over her head and went straight to sleep.

Chapter 29

MARIA SAT IN THE FRONT PASSENGER seat as William drove them all back to Oakside Grange feeling almost triumphant that they were taking their daughter back where she belonged. Emily could sense her mother's satisfaction and she inwardly squirmed, yet again, at her own catalogue of mistakes and failures. Every now and again Maria would pipe up with comments which were meant to comfort and reassure, yet all they did as far as Emily was concerned was make her feel naïve and gullible – someone who had been taken for an utter fool.

"Of course, none of us could ever see what you saw in him," she began when they were barely on the outskirts of Ilfracombe. "We just *knew* it could never last. Your dad and I have *never* liked him…"

And so it went on and there could be no question now that Emily's marriage to Darren O'Dowel was completely over. It had been totally exposed for the failure and sham that it was. Darren had seen to that when he slammed his way out of The Dunes, leaving his wife well and truly behind him. William grunted or nodded his agreement with Maria's comments whilst keeping focussed on the road ahead and Emily gazed at the rain patterns on her side window as she considered the pointlessness of her existence on this blackest of days. She was only grateful that neither her mum nor dad had brought up the subject of Darren's violence. Her upper lip was cut and there was a dark bruise just visible around her hairline on the right hand side of her face. Apart from that the bruises from last night were hidden either under her clothes or underneath her blonde hair. Emily spent the journey hovering on a knife edge of embarrassment, knowing how mortified and shamed she'd feel if the subject was brought up. Darren's violence towards her was something to be buried and hidden and kept to herself. It wasn't something to be talked about with her mum and dad – graphic images of her suffering providing them with pain and anguish that they didn't deserve. From Maria and William's point of view it was simply impossible to acknowledge what had so obviously taken place. In the darkest recesses of her mind Maria knew that if she acknowledged the fact that Darren had assaulted her precious daughter she may fall to pieces and never recover. As far as William was concerned it was completely beyond his comprehension that a man should attack and harm his wife. If he stayed focussed on the road ahead and lived solely for the here and now he would never have to face and tackle the questions that that cut lip and hair line bruise raised. So, on that long road journey back home the most prevalent thoughts on everyone's mind were left unspoken – Maria, William and Emily dealt with their own personal tortures in their own private ways.

The tensions they all felt erupted later that evening. Emily felt strangely hemmed in at Oakside Grange and was dying for a stiff drink and a smoke of some kind. She also felt angry that she had meekly gone back to her parent's home when by rights the house that she shared with Darren was half hers. Why shouldn't *he* find somewhere else to go to?

"For God's sake," Maria exploded when Emily aired her views, "I hope you're not thinking of going back there for the sake of some stupid principle! You can be a fool once but surely not for a second time!"

Emily burst into tears. "You just all think I'm stupid and foolish and a total failure! You always made out you *liked* Darren."

"Yes," Maria screamed, "For *your* sake you little idiot!"

William intervened before the accusations and recriminations could get out of hand.

"Now come on both of you, this is getting us absolutely nowhere. It's pointless going over what's already happened and why... let's think of the future... Emily's future.... of the best way forward from here..."

"I'm going to put the kettle on," muttered Emily and she headed for the kitchen praying that the bottle of whiskey kept purely for medicinal purposes was still there. Maria and William rarely drank alcohol apart from special occasions and weren't the kind of people to keep a well stocked drinks cabinet. She opened the food cupboard and pushed aside some packets of rice and pasta. Bingo! There it was lurking at the back and what's more it was three quarters full. She found some lemonade in the fridge and poured out a stiff measure of whiskey for herself and two much weaker ones for her parents. Their forced inclusion would save her from the awkwardness of drinking alone.

"Whiskey, lemonade and ice!" she announced as she presented the three tumblers on a tray back in the living room. "Let's drink to the best way forward."

Emily sipped at her drink continuously whilst William's and Maria's remained largely untouched. Trying to be constructive, William suggested that a respected firm of solicitors he knew via his work may be worth talking to about the legal side of the separation.

"What about Rocket Sound?" asked Emily who had become tearful again. "What about my job? I'm going to lose it aren't I?"

"It's unfair, love," said William, "But I can't honestly see how you can carry on there... Is there someone who you work with who you can call tomorrow and explain the situation to them?"

"Lenny... the head of commercial production..."

"Well, put a call through to this Lenny chap first thing... see what he's got to say about it. I'll give Macintosh & Co a call to see about a solicitor."

Maria was shocked to see that Emily had not only downed her own drink but was now starting on William's unwanted one.

"Come on," she said, briskly, "Your bed's all made up so why don't you get a good night's sleep? It's been a long day and you must be exhausted."

Emily agreed and made an awkward exit from the room, still uncomfortable in the role of 'little girl back home'.

Maria and William stayed up, talking over the events of the day in hushed tones, questioning whether they could have done something to prevent the relationship from developing yet always coming to the same old conclusions.

"All we can do," said William, "Is make it better from here on in. What's done is done and Emily's got to start afresh. She's home now love," he said, putting his arms around Maria. "Let's just thank God that she's home."

Emily was in their empty lounge, crawling around in circles on all fours. She couldn't get up and nor could she stop herself going round and round and round. She was tired and confused but her limbs kept forcing her around this circular path. The room was in semi darkness but Emily could clearly make out that the shelves were void of any ornaments or trinkets. There were no pictures on the walls either and the settee had been stripped down to its base. As she continued her journey round and round she noticed some of the paint peel away from the walls. Then some of the plaster followed, dissolving in front of her eyes, exposing the brick work beneath. Her journey became slower, her movements sluggish. There was a weight bearing down on her back and she looked over her shoulder to see Darren riding her as if astride a horse.

"You're too slow," he laughed, "You need whipping!"

He threw back his head and cackled like a witch before leaning forward and bringing his chest down onto her back.

"Please forgive me Emily… I've got a surprise for you. Then everything will be alright, you'll see."

"You're not making sense, Darren," said Emily, "You're just not making sense…"

She gagged as Darren put his hand over her mouth, ramming a fist full of spiders on top of her tongue and down her throat. She tried to spit out the hateful black creatures but Darren was forcing her to swallow them. She tried to beg but there were too many spiders in her mouth for her to speak.

She couldn't speak and now she couldn't breath. He was suffocating her. The spiders he'd forced into her mouth were choking her to death.

Emily screamed and sprang up out of her bed, clawing at her mouth and tongue. She sank down to her knees and gasped for breath taking in huge gasps of air. Maria and William ran up the stairs and found her, retching and sobbing with her head in her hands.

Chapter 30

"**Well, Emily, I think I can** safely say that you're suffering from depression."

It was the day before Christmas Eve and Emily was Dr Ellen Edmond's last patient before the surgery closed for the evening.

"I'm going to prescribe you a course of anti-depressants and see how you get on. You've been through an awful lot my dear, so lets get you back on track, shall we?"

Emily nodded and thanked Christ that she'd finally been able to tell someone that the pain of merely existing in this world was threatening to overwhelm and destroy her. Dr Edmonds busied herself writing out a prescription and hoped that her professional diagnosis would start to mend this broken young lady who sat in front of her. Of course the rot had set in with the death of her younger brother - that was text book stuff, page one... then an unsuitable marriage at such a young age... not to mention an excessive intake of alcohol on a regular basis. Well, it was simply no wonder that the girl had such a strong desire to go to sleep and never wake up!

Stepping out of the surgery Emily felt like skipping down the road and shouting to the world, *I'm depressed! I'm not going mad, I'm just depressed!*

The profound relief that her black thoughts, dark moods and lethargy had a label which could now be officially attached to them was making her feel better already, even before the course of medication began. It was about a half mile walk from the surgery back to Oakside Grange and it was already pitch black and bitterly cold. At this moment in time however Emily almost relished the solitude the return walk provided. It gave her a chance to think; to clear her mind and think of her life as it stood at this point. It had been a painful time since returning from Devon, yet now, since talking to Dr Edmonds, it seemed like there was some light at the end of the tunnel. She had dragged herself to the 'phone on the Monday morning and asked Lenny if he could cover for her for the rest of the week as she didn't feel up to coming in. She gave him a brief summary of what had happened and the fact that she and Darren had effectively spilt up. She heard him mutter 'bastard' under his breath before assuring her that he would undertake to write the scripts that came in to Commercial Production that week. Not being able to stand the uncertainty of her situation any longer she found herself blurting out that she assumed he would have to start looking for someone else, as for obvious reasons it would be impossible for her to work in the same building as Darren, especially as he was due to become part of the management team. But Lenny told her not to rush to any conclusions, to take the week off and he would call her by the end of it to see if she was OK.

As for any contact with Darren, she didn't call him and he didn't call her. Now the break had been made she wanted to shut him out of her life completely. She was due to see a solicitor the following week anyway and hopefully everything could go through him. It was via Lenny therefore that she heard news of Darren's immediate future. With undisguised glee he rang Emily to inform her that Darren had not been offered the managerial position after all. Apparently he'd been so fired up with rage that he'd resigned on the spot. Rocket Sound were going to make him work out a notice until Christmas and in the new year Darren was to move to Birmingham to help his old friend Michael Sheldon set up a recording studio. In light of this new development Lenny suggested that Emily stay out of the way until January at which

The End of Emily West

time she could resume her job as Commercial Script Writer with no fear of coming face to face with Darren O'Dowel.

The prospect of keeping her job had been a huge relief but Emily had come to realise that her time with Darren had left her with scars that would take a long time to heal. Each day brought fresh waves of hatred, resentment and self doubt and each night held the promise of another sickening dream. She wanted to bury the memory of Darren in a deep pit without the chance of it ever surfacing, but of course that was impossible. If her solicitor, Mr Rhodes, was to do his job properly he required every minute detail of her marriage, and whilst it was proving somewhat therapeutic to write down for him some of the violence she had endured, it was a far cry from her wish to bury the subject deep underground.

It was the week before Christmas that Mr Rhodes passed on to her a letter from Darren which had been posted to his office.

"I'm obliged to give you this," he said, "But I want you to know that I've already written back to Mr O'Dowel's solicitor and said that the answer is a definite 'no'. The fact is Emily, he wants you back."

Emily returned home, shut herself in her bedroom and poured a large glass of whiskey and ginger from her supply in the bedside cupboard before reading Darren's letter.

Emily cried as she read it. She didn't want to and hadn't thought she would, but she did. On the face of it no one who read such a letter could fail to be moved by it; such an outpouring of sorrow and remorse, of promises to try harder, to love and cherish her forever. Emily had hated the rollercoaster of emotions she'd been subjected to as Darren's wife and this was more of the same; the 'high' of feeling that things were going to change for the better, always to be followed by the stomach churning plummet to the depths of despair. She folded the letter back up and returned it to its envelope. Thank goodness that Mr Rhodes had taken the pressure away from her to respond. They'd got on straightaway and Joe Rhodes was becoming increasingly instrumental in giving back to Emily just some of the huge amount of confidence she had lost in her role as Mrs O'Dowel.

Christmas and the whole of the festive season that year was one of the most pleasant Emily could remember for some time…. maybe those anti-depressants were starting to do their job. Quite apart from that there was no treading on egg shells, no scurrying around like a frightened rabbit, no waiting on Darren hand and foot and bowing to his every idea, mood and whim. She took Cocoa out for long walks whenever she liked and spent hours down at Whitemoor Farm tending to Rascal's every need. This year the Christmas and New Year celebrations were as they should be; television repeats and The Wizard of Oz, nuts and Satsumas and boxes of chocolates, daft games and cheap table crackers, silly hats and bad jokes and a never ending stream of relations to entertain and friends to go crazy with. Emily even went out with Lenny and some more of the staff at Rocket Sound for some post Christmas and pre New Year drinks. Emily assumed that Lenny had given orders for the subject of Darren O'Dowel to be avoided as no one probed too much into the finer details of her current situation. She could sense however that Darren had not been a popular member of the Rocket Sound team. How the scales were falling from her eyes… all that time of assuming that the people who worked at Rocket looked up to Darren O'Dowel – respected him, sought out his opinion, craved his approval. What a mug she'd been. What an utter fool. But how satisfying to discover that Darren wasn't the popular, highly regarded figure he'd thought himself to be.

Julie from Sales raised her glass to her lips but stopped half way to let out an exaggerated groan.
"Oh, God Almighty! Look who's just walked in!"
All eyes turned to the wine bar entrance in time to see Mel Green saunter over to the bar.
"Who the fuck told her we were having a few drinks here tonight?" Julie demanded.
"You mean *Mel*?" asked Emily, aware that she was missing something.
"Sorry Emily, forgot you'd been away," said Anthony from Accounts. "The fact is, it would appear that our Mel has firmly taken on the position of 'station bike'… not that I've had a ride you understand…"

Julie burst out laughing. "You and the happily married Lenny are about the only ones! Most of the boys at Rocket had a mass excursion to the clap clinic last week courtesy of Ms Green!"

Banter and whispers and gossip abounded before Julie changed the subject completely by complaining loudly about the mean Christmas bonuses all the full time staff had received that year. But Emily was still thinking about Mel Green becoming the station tart. At least Darren had never been unfaithful to her. Christ, she had been through some shit and he'd been the biggest bastard one could ever wish to meet but she had never for one minute had reason to suspect that he had cheated on her. Abusing her *and* cheating on her? Now the injustice of that really would be too much to bear.

Three nights later Emily found herself back at the same wine bar with Jackie Dean toasting in the New Year. Jackie's boyfriend had recently left her for his second cousin and she had spent most of the night telling Emily that all men were bastards and therefore she and Emily were definitely better off single… well, for a while at least. Emily tended to agree that it would be nice to be young, free and single again but she was gratified to come to the conclusion that Darren O'Dowel hadn't put her off men altogether. Yes, it would be so easy to become bitter and cynical, cold and untrusting but if Darren left her with that legacy then his power over her would be everlasting. And more than anything else, Emily wanted to put the appalling Darren years behind her and move on. Everyone in the wine bar joined in the countdown to midnight and on the count of zero they all clapped and cheered and clinked their glasses together. Emily and Jackie did the same with their two full glasses of house white before lighting up a celebratory Silk Cut apiece.

"Happy New Year, Emily" shouted Jackie.

"Happy New Year to you too, Jackie," Emily shouted back. "May we both find fame and fortune and two rich and handsome men!"

"Hah! I'll drink to that!"

In those first few minutes of January 1st Emily and Jackie talked of the year ahead; of hopes and dreams, of fantasies and ambitions. Like all other New Year revellers it never entered their heads to predict doom and tragedy, to anticipate misery or pain. Why should it? They were young and free and had the world at their feet. Who knew what the next year would bring?

Chapter 31

She was Cocoa and Cocoa was *her. This fusion of beings took on the physical form of the dog yet this chocolate Labrador was no longer young. This new version of Cocoa was weighty and sluggish. Her coat was dull and her breaths came out in heavy, laboured pants. She raised her head as a shadow fell over her. It was Darren. Darren was a vet and she was lying on a table in his surgery. One hand reached down to stroke her face. The other hand held a syringe. The pure terror that she felt rendered her unable to make a sound although inside she was screaming for him to stop. Death was a certainty now, for undoubtedly the syringe contained the necessary medication to put her to sleep. Darren selected a patch of her furry skin and plunged in the needle but instead of the blackness she'd anticipated there was dazzling sunlight and she found herself in the field at Whitemoor Farm. Mr Johnson threw a tennis ball for her, sending it up in a huge arc and down to the sycamore trees. Cocoa's limbs were no longer worn and old and her previously lacklustre coat was now silken and positively glistening in the fierce light. She ran after the ball. She was young again – young and free. On she ran, on and on and on, faster and faster until she thought she might run forever.*

Emily's eyes snapped open and she found herself on the floor by the side of the bed, the bedding in a crumpled heap around her. She was breathing heavily and was hot and damp with sweat. *Darren with a syringe. Darren coming to get her and Cocoa.* Cocoa ambled over and thrust his dry nose into her face, wondering why his sleep had been disturbed. Emily hugged him and wondered how long the memory of Darren O'Dowel was to haunt her.

By the end of January Emily had got into the swing of things back at Rocket Sound, Darren was in Birmingham working at Michael Sheldon's recording studio and their former marital home was about to be put up for sale. Neither party had any interest, or indeed the wherewithal, to buy the other out so all that remained was for the property to be sold and the two sides to argue over the division of equity and assets. Emily had kept to her strict policy of having no personal contact with Darren, although he had recently requested, via Mr Rhodes, that they meet 'face to face' to discuss the division of some jointly owned household goods. Emily didn't need to see Darren face to face – he was constantly in her thoughts and persistently invading her dreams, like a painful, nagging wound that refused to heal.

On Saturday afternoon Emily went down to Whitemoor Farm to muck out Rascal's stable and to check the fit of a newly purchased New Zealand rug. It was getting dark by the time she'd nearly finished her chores and the voice that seemed to come from nowhere out of the twilight gave her a start.

"I guessed I might find you down here…"

She turned and peered out over the stable door. "Hello…?"

"Hello, Emily."

He came right up to the door and they stood staring at each other, standing not two feet apart.

"*Paul!*"

"Yep, and all ready to whisk you away from the muck heap and take you down to the pub for a drink! I might even throw in some pub grub."

"Paul Andrew! I can't *believe* it! What are you *doing* here? You're meant to be in Australia! Anyway, aren't you several years too late? Weren't you coming back for me as soon as you were sixteen? Or was it eighteen, I can't remember!"

"Well, if only I had of done… I could have saved you from that rotten husband of yours! It's OK, I've had the full story from your mum… I called in at Oakside and your mum filled me in on all the gory details."

Emily groaned before letting herself out of the stable and hugging her old school sweetheart. God, he felt good. He felt good and he smelt good which was more then could be said for her at this moment in time. Paul wrinkled his nose in mock disgust.

"Please tell me you have some clean clothes to change into?!"

She laughed and linked her arm through his as she guided him towards the Johnson's cottage. She had clean clothes there… even a bit of make-up too. She could have a quick wash, pin her hair up…. She gazed up at Paul's face and felt a spring in her step that hadn't been there for years.

"My God, Emily, you can put it away, can't you?"

Paul was commenting on the fact that she was on her fifth whiskey and ginger whilst he was still finishing off his second pint of beer.

"Hah, I can drink most people under the table," she said, full of bravado and self confidence. "I've had tonnes of practice!"

During the course of the night they caught up with all the news of the past few years. They chatted and laughed and reminisced and Emily was almost sad to suddenly realise that being with Paul was like putting on a pair of favourite old pyjamas and snuggling up by the fire with a good book. Some kind of feelings were there but they were not the right ones. He was handsome and lovely and they kissed and cuddled at various points during the conversation but Emily couldn't find the necessary passion in her heart that might indicate a 'happy ever after' ending was possible. It was a relief therefore, when it became obvious as the night went on that Paul was not thinking along those lines either. He was happy in Australia and could never envisage coming back to live in England. His whole family had taken to the place like ducks to water and his parents often wondered why they hadn't made the move sooner than they did. Paul had a good job with wonderful prospects, a smart apartment and a true middle class lifestyle. The Andrews had reached out to Australia and Australia had welcomed them with open arms.

Inevitably they had got around to talking about Darren O'Dowel and how awful Emily's life had been with him.

"There is one blessing, Emily," said Paul, "Thank God you never had any children. At least you can make a clean break and you'll never have any need to see the wanker again."

Emily agreed that it was indeed a blessing that there wasn't a child on the scene to complicate matters and Paul went on to tell her about a work colleague of his who had recently become a father for the first time.

"You should see the poor bugger… bags under his eyes and too hen pecked to stay and have a drink after work. I tell you, we're too young to have kids… God, imagine the responsibility. At this point in my life I really can't think of anything worse. I'm going to bloody well live first before drowning in a sea of dirty nappies!"

When the pub closed for the night Paul walked Emily back to Oakside Grange.

"Come over here for lunch tomorrow," she said on impulse. "Mum and Dad are driving down to Birmingham for a couple of days to visit Aunt Mary. I'll cook, you bring the wine. It might be twenty years before I see you again!"

Paul happily accepted the invitation and bracing themselves against the freezing cold air, they kissed goodnight.

After a laid back Sunday lunch, some wine, a nap, an old film and some more wine it was the easiest and most obvious thing in the world for Emily to lead Paul up to her bedroom. Their naked bodies entwined under the sheets and Emily felt like she was justified in proving to herself that she could sleep with another man apart from Darren O'Dowel. Darren hadn't turned her into soiled goods – other men obviously did find her desirable and here she was proving just that. She didn't *fancy* Paul as such, but she loved him. He was part of her past and she would always love him. But she may not see him again for a very long time. He was travelling back home tomorrow, half way around the world and what better way to say goodbye than this? Much later on that night Paul left Oakside Grange. Both of them knew he would not return, just as they both knew that they were not destined to be together. His life was in Australia and Emily wished him luck as she hugged him close for the last time. He told her to take care of herself and she promised that she would. When she had waved him off she poured herself a large glass of whiskey and walked slowly upstairs to bed.

Darren was standing behind her. She couldn't see him but she knew it was him. He was standing so close that she could feel his breath on the back of her neck and his erection in the small of her back. 'You know you want it. Don't tell me you don't want it,' he whispered in her ear. She was paralysed with fear – the only part of her body she was able to move was her eyes. She lifted them to the sky. It was the sky above the sycamore trees at the bottom of the field at Whitemoor Farm. Rascal was standing underneath the tree and Mrs Johnson was sitting on his back. Mr Johnson was calling out but she couldn't see him. 'Look out, look out!' he cried and raising her eyes once more she saw an aeroplane flying dangerously low. It was a passenger plane, an airbus, and it was going to crash into the field. Darren pushed his erection harder into her back and moaned. She couldn't move. She stood rooted to the spot as the plane nosedived into the trees and huge shards of glass and metal came flying towards them. The debris made a thumping noise as it rocketed up the field and Emily screamed in horror at the devastation. Still the thumping noise continued and she looked down to see the glass cutting her legs to shreds. Darren called out, 'Emily, Emily!'

Emily woke up, crying and shivering. It was still dark outside although the bedside clock told her she had slept the whole night through and it was seven o'clock in the morning. Only a few seconds passed before she heard a series of loud knocks on the front door and Darren's voice shouting out her name. She crept out onto the hall landing and quickly looked out at the driveway below before drawing back and crouching down on the carpet. It was him. It was Darren.

He was here, knocking on the front door, ranting and raving and demanding to be let in so they could talk.

Go away, go away, go away.

Emily felt like a caged animal, with nowhere to hide and nowhere to run. That familiar feeling of being powerless and utterly helpless in the presence of Darren O'Dowel washed over her again and she sat on the carpet rocking backwards and forwards in a kind of trance until eventually, some twenty minutes later, Darren gave up his quest and went away.

Once Emily arrived at work she called Mr Rhodes and told him what had happened. His response was immediate and without question; he would apply for an emergency court injunction to keep Darren O'Dowel away from Emily West. Emily stared at her computer screen, trying to concentrate on the task in hand which was to write a thirty second commercial extolling the virtues of buying your bathroom from Making Waves Ltd. But the words wouldn't come and the screen stayed blank. Leaving her desk to seek inspiration at the coffee machine Emily wondered, yet again, when this living nightmare would end.

It was the middle of May when Emily finally came to the conclusion that she may be pregnant. Following the taking out of the court injunction at the end of January Darren had turned the divorce into a bloody and bitter battle of who should get what from the sale of the house. Her mind had been focussed on that or work and when neither of those subjects needed addressing her attention was taken by generous measures of whiskey and ginger.

Dr Edmonds swiftly confirmed her suspicions and she stumbled out of the surgery blinded by tears of frustration and confusion. The baby was Paul's – there was no doubt about that – but there was no need for Paul or anyone else to know that fact. Emily recalled how adamant he had been about not wanting the responsibility of children at this time in his life, so how could it possibly be fair to burden him with this turn of events? She thought back to the night they'd spent together and cursed them both for being so reckless and naïve. No pill and no condom, just irresponsible love making with the precaution of him pulling out at the last minute. Obviously that method had not worked. Her mind worked overtime until her head throbbed with the effort of trying to collate all the thoughts that were being pushed around, dismissed and then reconsidered. How was she going to tell her mum and dad? Their daughter had become pregnant and refused to name the father… another disastrous episode for them to deal with courtesy of her failure to function as a mature and responsible adult. More pieces for them to pick up, more strain and more disappointment. What about an abortion? It wasn't too late to go ahead with a termination. She wrestled with her conscience and lost the battle. She thought of Bobby and his little life which had been over before it had begun. He had fought to stay alive so how could she simply throw away the tiny life that was now growing inside her. Perhaps her parents would be pleased with the news… who knew what they would make of it? If only she could suspend time and bury her head deep in the sand so the problem needn't be addressed at all.

As if a knight in shining armour had ridden at breakneck speed towards her it was Lenny who offered Emily an immediate opportunity by which to delay dropping the bombshell on Oakside Grange. An ex-colleague of his who worked at River FM in London had let him know of a short term vacancy for a commercial scriptwriter. It was a short term contract and Lenny told Emily he felt duty bound to tell her about it.

"It's not that I want you to leave Rocket Sound," Lenny explained, "Far from it, in fact… but it did occur to me that with all the mess of the divorce etc it may do you good to have a change of scene for a little while… you know, get out there and have some fun! And of course it's a golden opportunity for you to dip your toe into the bright lights of London. We'd only replace you here with someone on a short contract so the option to come back would be here. My sister's in Richmond– West London, that is – and she sometimes rents out her fourth bedroom to people in the media. Whopping great house Jill and Jonathon have got… it's on Richmond Hill, if you're interested.…"

A thought fluttered into Emily's head; some words of wisdom that Jackie Dean had come out with the last time they'd met up.

"Do you know?" she'd asked Emily, "That most people in this world spend all their time regretting the past, worrying about the future and pissing all over today!"

Well that settled it; she was going to live for the moment. And on that fragile and somewhat dangerous premise Emily banished all thoughts of her parents, her baby and her future from her mind, embarked upon a drip feed of whiskey to dull her senses and floated off down to London. She'd finish at River FM at the end of August and then come home to reveal that the baby was due in the middle of October. It was a plan at least, a route forward. And beyond that? Well, she refused to give it any thought at all.

Chapter 32

EMILY SLID INTO LIFE AT RIVER FM like a hot knife through butter. She was also sailing through her pregnancy and turned out to be one of those expectant mothers who, with the aid of floaty summer dresses and loose fitting tops does not actually look pregnant at all. Also, no one at the station had any idea of what she normally looked like and if anything just assumed she was a rather bonny lass. This suited her extremely well as she didn't want any station gossip finding its way back up to Rocket Sound and ultimately to her parents. She'd tell them in her own time and in her own way which was at Oakside Grange at the end of August when her time at River FM would be over. Actually, during the month of August most of the people she worked with did finally clue on that she was pregnant but as far as she knew the gossip never found its way north of Watford. If it did then Lenny was too wise to bring up the subject when they spoke on the 'phone. The clinic she had registered with in London confirmed that all was well with mother and child and her new doctor prescribed her more anti-depressants to carry on the good work of the last batch. All in all Emily was beginning to feel pretty damn good, especially as those terrible nightmares she suffered from which always featured Darren were not happening nearly so often as they used to. The change of scene was like a tonic, a breath of fresh air and like any new resident in London she couldn't help but be intoxicated by its beauty and energy. She thought back to how badly she had once wanted to come to university here, to be dazzled by the bright lights and to tread the streets which were paved of gold. Well, here she was at last and the reality of London was proving to be even better than the dream.

That summer spent in the city held a magic that Emily had never encountered before. Being in London made her feel like anything was possible, that dreams had here could be fulfilled and that to cheer yourself up you only had to throw yourself into the melting pot of people and cultures that bubbled over to create this vibrant place. In no time at all Emily felt she was an old hand at the daily commute from Richmond to Waterloo. Her pocket London A-Z was with her at all times and she often took pleasure in simply looking at the map and pinpointing the exact location of world famous street names and landmarks. It never failed to give her a warm glow of satisfaction that she was actually here and could visit these places at any time she cared to choose. Never mind the heat and the dust or the sweaty journeys on over packed tube trains. Never mind the drug addicts and the beggars, never mind that the wrong turn down the wrong street may expose the dregs of humanity, never mind the stairwells and subways that stank of urine and were littered with fag packets and beer cans. Emily assumed that everyone who came to London was besotted by it - only had eyes for the bright and the beautiful; street entertainers in Covent Garden, river boats on the Thames, soldiers at Buckingham Palace, fairy lights outside The Ritz, the chimes of Big Ben and the Food Halls at Harrods. Those who want to be dazzled will be… those who don't will be forever disillusioned and get left behind.

In the height of the summer, on the anniversary of Bobby's death, Emily spent a good part of the evening sitting quietly, resolving that one day she would return to this city which she had fallen so completely in love with. She was back in Richmond, leaning back on a bench at the top of the Terrace Gardens on Richmond Hill. She was gazing out over one of the most expensive and desirable views in any of the London boroughs; the curve of the Thames as it flowed through the Petersham Meadows below. Property overlooking this commanded prices that made the average person wince and understandably therefore it was the domain of rock stars, stock brokers and Arab sheiks. But Emily had ambition. This view was going to be hers one day. This or the red roof tops of Knightsbridge where Harrods and Harvey Nichols became your local shops. Or maybe the view of the houseboats at Chelsea, seen from a mansion flat on Cheyne Walk. She may even be tempted by one of those newly converted warehouses which looked up the river towards Tower Bridge. It was all here for the taking and on this particular anniversary she felt she owed it to Bobby to *do* something with her life. She ran her hands over the neat bulge of her stomach. A new life… and a little bit of Bobby would live on because of it.

Three weeks later Emily was slowly packing up her things, preparing to return home the following week. She had missed her mum and dad and had felt mean when she had put them off coming down to London to visit her during the summer. Well, now she was going to go home and make things right. She'd grown up and she'd grown stronger and with this baby on its way it was about time too. Being pregnant had even curbed her desire for alcohol, making her skin clear and luminous and her eyes brighter and more alert. Her senses were no longer dulled and she felt ready to take on the world.

It was in the morning, two days before she was due to go home that she walked out of the Richmond Hill house and Darren stepped out in front of her.

"Gotcha!" he laughed.

"Darren!" Emily felt her legs go weak and her skin flush. Her throat tightened and she felt fear rising up inside her. She thanked God that she was wearing a voluminous old Mac because it was threatening rain. The thought of Darren knowing she was pregnant made her feel sick.

"You're not supposed to come near me," she started, "The Court Injunction…"

"Oh, *come on*, Emily, I think we're a bit past all that rubbish aren't we?"

His voice and manner remained unthreatening and an easy smile stayed fixed on his face. His face was puffy and pink, with either too much drink or too much sun, Emily couldn't tell. His jeans were crumpled and worn and his white t-shirt was grubby and old. He saw

Emily clocking his appearance and quickly apologised for his state of dress.

"Been up most the night helping with the refurbishment of a voice-over studio in Putney… had to be up and running by this morning.…"

"What about Birmingham?" Emily asked, frozen to the spot, at a loss for anything to say.

"Oh, couldn't be better. Michael and I have built up that recording business from nothing you know. The building itself was practically derelict before we began. Look, I've got some pictures in the car…"

Darren turned to the hire car they were standing by and opened the driver's door. Emily assumed he was going to reach inside for the photographs but instead he grabbed hold of her, yanked her in front of him and pushed her roughly into the car. It was so sudden and so shocking that Emily didn't have time to shout or scream. She could only gasp with horror and try to protect her baby as she was propelled into the front passenger seat. Darren jumped in, turned the ignition and central locked the doors and in a matter of seconds they were driving off towards Richmond Park.

All Emily's senses told her to panic but she knew she had to stay calm if she was to gain some kind of control. Even so, when she spoke her voice was little more than a strangled cry.

"How did you find me?"

"I followed you home last night from River FM. I bumped into Mel Green last week and she told me about your cushy little job down here in London. You didn't believe that shit about me working in Putney last night, did you?"

"I don't know what to think… we've both moved on Darren, haven't we? If we can just agree about the money from the house… and you've got a brilliant job in Birmingham…"

"Fuck you!" Darren shouted and he punched Emily in the mouth with the back of his fist. She screamed and put her hands up to her face, realising that they were now in the Park itself taking the road towards Kingston Gate. To the fury of the other road users, cyclists and joggers Darren was completely ignoring the twenty mile per hour speed limit.

"Where are we going?" she sobbed, "Where are we going?"

"We're going on a magical fucking mystery tour while I tell you how you've ruined my life you fucking little *cow*. There is no pissing job in Birmingham, not any more. The whole thing was a fucking fiasco. I could have been a manager at Rocket by now if it hadn't been for you poisoning them all against me."

He was ranting and shouting as he turned the car into the car park at Pembroke Lodge and spun it round on the gravel to drive back towards Richmond Gate where they'd come in. He was driving but Emily could tell he wasn't seeing anything on the road in front of him.

"Please, Darren, *please*... I swear to God I had nothing to do with that. Please, Darren, just stop the car and we can talk. Where are we going? Where are you taking me? You'll get us both killed like this."

"Haven't you got it yet, *Mrs O'Dowel*? That's exactly what I'm fucking well planning on."

Darren screeched the car into a left turn out of Richmond Gate and picked up speed down the hill towards Petersham. By the time he jumped an orange light at the next junction they were travelling at sixty five miles an hour. They car approached the sharp left bend where the road narrows by Rutland Lodge at over seventy five miles an hour and there wasn't a chance that they weren't going to crash. As Darren lost control and Emily stared out of the windscreen, mute with horror, the Kingston to Richmond double decker bus was approaching the bend from the opposite direction.

There was no time to think of anything. No time for screams or cries of anguish, for regrets or tears. There was simply no time left, just the point of impact and an instant wall of black.

Darren O'Dowel succumbed immediately to his crash induced injuries.

Emily West was still alive, but slowly losing the fight.

Chapter 33

MR AND MRS JOHNSON SAT QUIETLY in St Matthew's church, waiting for the service to begin. Mr Johnson was wearing a dark suit with a bright red tie and Mrs Johnson was wearing her best purple coat over a lilac floral dress. Maria had specifically asked them to wear bright colours because she so wanted this day to be a true celebration. Mrs Johnson checked her handbag again to make sure her pack of tissues was still there. Celebration or not there was going to be tears.

Jackie Dean was already fighting back all kinds of emotions. She was wearing shocking pink from head to toe and had a vision of Emily roaring with laughter at this recreation of Barbie. She briefly wondered if Darren was looking up at them all from his pit of fire… he was going to rot in hell, there was no doubt about that.

Lenny sat in a pew at the back with his head in his hands, wondering yet again how different things would have been if he hadn't have told Emily about the job in London. *What if, what if, what if?* He had loved working with Emily… they had shared such good times together. Was he partly to blame for what had happened on that fateful day? It would take him a very long time to find a satisfactory answer to that question.

The End of Emily West

Maria walked into St Matthew's on that cold February morning carrying what the local newspapers had emotionally referred to as a 'miracle'; a baby boy, father unknown and a miraculous survivor from Darren's crumpled wreck of a car by Rutland Lodge at the end of August. There hadn't been a hope that the baby would live and Maria and William often wondered if it was down to sheer will power that he had... endless days sitting by his incubator, willing him to pull through... weeks of praying for him to put on weight, to breathe on his own. He had been so very tiny, so frail and vulnerable and now here he was, small for his age yet smiling and gurgling and with a shock of blonde hair that reminded Maria so very much of Bobby when he was a baby. Today's Christening of him was a celebration they had thought may never come, yet here this little mite was like a shining ray of hope in all their lives, another chance of happiness.

William entered the church behind Maria, pushing the wheelchair which his daughter had been confined to since leaving hospital just before Christmas. Emily took a deep breath and fought to stay focussed, feeling that she might have turned and run if only her legs would have carried her. She had battled for life and now she faced the battle to *live* – to put an end to the old Emily, to banish the shadows, the pain and the fear and to start her life again. Darren was gone, but it would be a long, long time before he was forgotten.

They made their way to the front of the church and suddenly the silence was broken by spontaneous cheers and laughter. Emily looked around at the happy, expectant faces; Aunty Bea and Aunty Mary, Mr and Mrs Johnson, Aunt Fiona and Uncle Daniel, Jackie Dean and Barbra Ellery. Friends and family had turned out in force to show their love and support.

The baby began to cry. Emily smiled and put her hand up to him and rubbed his cheek. Maria cradled him tightly to her chest before placing him on Emily's knee. One chapter had ended and a new one was about to begin.

Little Robert West... a beautiful baby boy that any mother would be proud of.

A final note of thanks...

When it comes to domestic violence, happy endings cannot be taken for granted. Emily West was lucky to have friends and family around her who could help her get over the trauma of an abusive relationship. I was also lucky in that respect. Now being a parent myself I can only image the agony that my mum and dad went through over a six year period, wondering if their youngest daughter was lost to them forever. This would, therefore, seem like an appropriate point to thank my parents and also my sister for 'picking up the pieces'.

Printed in the United Kingdom by
Lightning Source UK Ltd., Milton Keynes
142205UK00001B/50/P